TOUCHSTONE

THE INNER PROMISE

Paths to Self-Perfection
by
SRI CHINMOY

A TOUCHSTONE BOOK
PUBLISHED BY SIMON AND SCHUSTER

If I can stop one heart from breaking, by Emily Dickinson, from *The Poems of Emily Dickinson,* Thomas H. Johnson, ed., is reprinted by permission of the publishers: The Belknap Press of Harvard University Press, Cambridge. Copyright © 1951, 1954 by the President and Fellows of Harvard College, and by permission of the trustees of Amherst College.

Frontispiece appears through the courtesy of
Fleet Press Corporation.

Copyright © 1974 by Sri Chinmoy
Copyright © 1972 by Sri Chinmoy Lighthouse
Copyright © 1971 by Sri Chinmoy Centre, Inc.
A Touchstone Book
Published by Simon and Schuster
A Gulf + Western Company
Rockefeller Center, 630 Fifth Avenue
New York, New York 10020

DESIGNED BY JACK JAGET
Manufactured in the United States of America

2 3 4 5 6 7 8 9 10

Library of Congress Cataloging in Publication Data

Chinmoy.
    The inner promise

    (A Touchstone book)

    1. Spiritual life.   I. Title
BL624.C465   294.5′44   74–9552
ISBN 0–671–21801–8 Casebound
ISBN 0–671–21720–8 Paperback

Sri Chinmoy
While standing there
Is at once vulnerable and invulnerable.

Vulnerable to receive
The aspiration of his devoted adherents.

Invulnerable by his purity
While weeding our souls.

Sri Chinmoy
Is the voyager who has come from God . . .
And by his eyes tells us about the God within us.

His sound is from the voice of the reed.
It seems to come from very far off . . .
The defined edge of his universe.

He gives form to invisible inspiration
Which through him finds manifestation.

His blessing
His touch
The emanations from his body
Cast off colors of the astral infinite
And resound off the ground he carefully walks on.

He takes care to awaken the soul
Gently
Like thunder from the distance which promises rain
To the parched earth.

We who have waited
Greet Guru
And ask if we may come in.

—PAUL JENKINS

Contents

5

MY ROSE PETALS

Foreword

The teachings and writings of the Master Sri Chinmoy are most revealing manifestations of the Supreme's way of guiding souls, unaspiring as well as aspiring, towards the goal of the beyond—the goal of infinite Light, Truth and Bliss.

When I read the Master's books, I better understand my life's purpose and my duty towards mankind. In Sri Chinmoy's Light, I see myself striving to serve, constantly and unconditionally, the Will of the Supreme Father.

—*Devadip* CARLOS SANTANA

To have been asked to write a short preface to a book by Sri Chinmoy is for me a great honour.

Sri Chinmoy, for the last four years, has been my guiding light both inwardly and outwardly. Here is a being who has realised and revealed and is continuously manifesting God's Transcendental Reality, which is Love, most pure, most sublime.

The height of consciousness which Sri Chinmoy has attained must be manifested in every moment of his being and doing. The words in this book, and indeed in all of Sri Chinmoy's books, are purely and simply embodied Divine Light. Consequently, to read—or better still to meditate on—the writings of Sri Chinmoy can do nothing but shed God's Light and Love on the deepest questions of human and divine life.

—*Mahavishnu* JOHN MCLAUGHLIN

Preface

Inspiration is not a contemporary word. It seems to belong to a faded dispensation, or, if used at all today, it is applied to artists who by some special gift are still able to experience a sudden heightening of their abilities. We ordinary mortals of the twentieth century, however, appear not only uninspired, but uninspirable. It is a result of the pace and density of modern urban life, we say, the routines of our labor and the clamor of our leisure, that we have seen inspiration fall away from us.

Though not our need for it. Each of us in his or her own way seeks in some form an increase of spirit. *Inspiration* means literally to breathe into. The Bible's vision of man's creation records the primal act of inspiration: God breathes his breath (*spiritus*) into his clay. Inspiration transforms. All through human history man has sought ways of inspiration, honored his longing to be awakened, to be transformed from one state to another. That longing is still with us, fiercely perennial. The need for inspiration is part of our nature. So, too, our capacity for it.

This need and capacity of our nature are of supreme value. They attest to the survival in us of the many-leveled relation between our energies and the energies outside ourselves. We are beings in context: physiologically we need air, psychologically we need to respond and to be responded to. On both levels the essence of our sense of being alive involves our experience of receiving, and in that receiving the feeling of fullness.

It is a high truth that it is better to give than to receive. Perhaps it is also true that it is impossible to give without receiving. Nothing comes from nothing; only from a fullness may we offer ourselves. Consciously or unconsciously our behavior bears witness to that principle. It is vital for us to be filled and we seek the means.

Moreover, though we might think receiving was in some way instinctual, it appears to be an instinct which may be diseased. Many of us are obsessive givers, but rarely permit the gift of letting another give to us. This is the pattern of much of our mis-loving. It is easier to say "I love you" than to hear it. Like the act of listening, being loved demands an openness, even a vulnerability. To some of us, such an openness may feel acutely difficult. We are defensive, and only guardedly permit something to enter us, a thought, a feeling, the life of another.

But we need to receive. We need the flow of breath, the circulation of response. And if this is true on physical and interpersonal planes, it is true, as well, on more subtle levels. *Beauty* is becoming a dog-eared word. *Beautiful* has become a cliché in our culture, yet perhaps the very frequency with which we apply the word attests to the persistence of our hunger for beauty's genuine inspiration. It is not that the sources of beauty are vanishing from us; on their profoundest levels such sources have always been in our presence and in ourselves. What appears to be decreasing is our ability to be inspired by beauty.

Like beauty, inspiration may come from everywhere and anywhere when we are open. So it becomes for some a question of the utmost urgency whether we can relearn or repossess our capacity to experience inspiration. Is inspiration ultimately a matter of grace? Or are there ways—once we have admitted the need to ourselves—to open to what may inspire?

In some ways the answer is contained in the question. "Once we have admitted the need to ourselves." The word *admit* has a kind of double meaning here: it means to confess and also to let in. Admission is itself an act of receiving, and when we admit something to ourselves we are actually opening ourselves to a new source of awareness.

From a psychological point of view this makes perfectly good sense; in effect what we are doing in admitting our need is accepting something about ourselves which we had previously not been willing to accept. Thus we have repossessed ourselves of an energy, an awareness, a feeling, rightfully integral to us. We begin, then, with admitting our need.

It is, in some ways, our most radical act.

From that admission, if it is sincere, a new openness will flow. Consciously and unconsciously we will begin to seek out sources of nourishment to feed our need. That seeking is aspiration's first call. We aspire to be inspired; we seek to move into relation with possible sources of energy and light. We will find ourselves stopping before new windows, hearing things that had been in the air all the time but which we had never noticed before. And we may turn to books with a new eagerness.

One such book might well be this one. How might you find out? By reading it. Yes, but there is the question of how. Surely not like a novel. There is no plot here. Nor is it like a usual book of essays, for these pieces are not arguments, not acts of reasoning or persuasion. Nor like informal talks transcribed and arranged, for though many of the prose pieces in this volume were originally delivered as talks, they are not casual or chatty. In fact, it will be immediately apparent that this writing is in some sense decidedly difficult. Capitalized abstractions are likely to strike our eye immediately. Sentences appear tautological. The voice we hear in this writing, in the prose at least, seems to speak *ex cathedra*. Inspiration may be here, but how to receive it?

It may be helpful to know something of the man who spoke and wrote these words and the conditions under which they were heard.

Sri Chinmoy was born in Bengal, India, in 1931. At a very early age he began those meditative practices which perfected him in self-knowledge. He came to the United States in 1964, worked for the Indian Consulate and gradually drew to himself people who felt his power and light. The number of such people who have been drawn to him has grown steadily over the decade. His has by no means been a wildfire popularity, and though today he has meditation centers in Europe, in Canada and throughout the United States, his following is not large. Only those who are ready for him, for his purity, his intensity and his height, does Sri Chinmoy call disciples. But in his writing, his lectures and public meditations, he makes himself fully available to both the aspiring and the curious. Every year he travels to Europe and to campuses in America and Canada, speaking to audiences small and large, providing inspiration for those who can receive it.

Each of the pieces in this book was delivered to such an audience. Each talk was preceded by silence, the silence not of a speaker waiting for his listeners to settle, but of a meditation master filling a room with his stillness and peace. All Sri Chinmoy's talks emerge directly from high meditative states; they bear the fullness of his highest consciousness. For that reason they require from us more than the usual act of passive reading. We must enter into, admit, as best we can the consciousness that is in these pages. Sri Chinmoy speaks slowly. His voice is musical. Often his sentences spin brief harmonic patterns. He never talks for very long, always spontaneously. Always his words point to feelings, point to possibilities of awareness; they map out or evoke states of consciousness, aspects of our nature and condition which offer us a clearer sense of identity.

How, then, might we come to his words on the page before us? First we must let ourselves become still. It will not do to rush at his words with a mind buzzing from the noise of the day. It will not help to have a sharp pencil in our hands. It would be good to close our eyes for a moment. To take some measured breaths, letting the breath come more quietly. Perhaps we are sitting comfortably. Alone. The TV set is not on. The radio is not on. The record player is not on. We have admitted some silence. Then let that openness which led you to take up the book in the first place surface in yourself again. Trust that what you are about to read is something you need to hear, though you may not "understand." Let the book open to any page, let your eyes fall where they will. Hear the words in your heart, slowly. Do not question; listen.

Reading Sri Chinmoy is possible only as an act of meditation. As such what is important is the quality, not the duration, of the act. In reading him we are advised to persist only as long as we are feeling receptive. We may read no more than three or five minutes. We may find we have paused, hovered, over a phrase and that it has repeated itself in our mind. Or we may find the intrusions of thoughts push the writing out of our attention; and we may strain to pit the writing against distractions to din them out. This will not work. Do not force the writing upon your mind; better to close the book and return another time.

Only under such circumstances may the writing be given its chance to breathe. This writing is an invitation to a dance. It will lead us, if we dispose ourselves; however, without our assent and sincerity, its grace will elude us. The experience of such reading is unique. As a friend of mine has written: "Making friends with the written words of a genuine soul-master is as delicate and rewarding as making friends with the master himself, because his words are not simply tools for the expression of intellectual knowledge, but the living seeds of spirituality: seeds which germinate in the heart center—the center from which we love, not in the center of calculation."

These words come from that center. May you feel their inspiration.

Brihaspati Dr. Peter
Pitzele
*Associate Professor of English,
Brooklyn College*

EASTERN LIGHT FOR THE WESTERN MIND

SPIRITUALITY:
WHAT IT IS AND WHAT IT IS NOT

University of the West Indies, Kingston, Jamaica

January 10, 1968

Spirituality is man's boundless freedom in his life-boat: the freedom of his life-journey, the freedom from his life-pangs and the freedom beyond his life-achievements.

In spirituality is man's farthest Vision. In spirituality is man's nearest reality. God has Compassion. Man has aspiration. Spirituality is the consciousness-light that unites man's aspiration and God's Compassion. Spirituality tells man that he is God veiled and that God is man revealed.

Spirituality is not an escape from the world of reality. Spirituality tells us what the true reality is and how we can discover it here on earth. Spirituality is not the denial of life, but the purest acceptance of life. Life is to be accepted unreservedly. Life is to be realized soulfully. Life is to be transformed totally. Life is to be lived eternally.

Spirituality is not the song of ignorance. It is the mother of concentration, meditation and realization. Concentration takes me dynamically to God. Meditation silently brings God to me. Realization neither takes me to God nor brings God to me. Realization reveals to me that God is the Bluebird of Infinity's Reality and I am the Golden Wings of Divinity's Truth.

Spirituality has taught me the difference between my speech and my silence, between my mind and my heart. In speech I try to become. In silence I am. When I open my mouth, God closes my heart. When I close my mouth, God opens my heart. My mind says, "God needs me." My heart says, "I need God." My mind wants to possess God's Creation while negating it. My heart wants to embrace God's Creation while serving it. My mind says it does not know whether it thinks of God or of itself. At times my mind feels that since it does not think of God, neither does God think of it. My heart sees and feels that God thinks of it even if it does not care to think of God.

Spirituality has told me secretly what my supreme necessity is and how I can have it. What is my supreme necessity? God's Blessing. How can I have it? By simply borrowing it from God's Bank.

How can I pay off my debt? Easily! Just by borrowing once again from God's Bank. But I must borrow wisdom and nothing else. Wisdom possessed, debt nullified. Verily, this wisdom is the breath of spirituality.

I am God's experiment. He has given me my name: Science. I am God's experience. He has given me my name: Spirituality. I am God's Realization. He has given me my name: Oneness—Oneness within, Oneness without.

God is my Reality.
Heaven is my Immortality.
Earth is my Divinity.

On earth I grow.
With heaven I become.
In God I am.

FEAR OF THE INNER LIFE

University of the West Indies, Kingston, Jamaica
January 12, 1968

Strange is this world of ours. Stranger is our human understanding. Strangest is our fear of the inner life.

Most of us do not know what the inner life is. What is the inner life? It is the life that lives to grow and grows to live. It grows in the unhorizoned vision of the soul. It lives in the sublimest plenitude of the soul. This inner life always acts in accordance with the transforming and fulfilling light of the soul. If you do not know your soul, then in the world of divine wisdom you will be accused of dire ignorance. When you know your soul, in no time you become acquainted with God.

Please do not be forgetful of your great promise to God. Before you came into the world, before you donned the human cloak, you told God, your sweet Lord, with all the sincerity at your command, that you would participate in His divine *lila* (Drama). He said to you, "My child, fulfill Me and fulfill yourself at the same time on earth." You were divinely thrilled; your joy knew no bounds. You said, "Father, I shall. May my soulful promise be worthy of Your compassionate Command."

As ill-luck would have it, you have now totally forgotten your promise. Here on earth you want to fulfill not God, but yourself. Your unlit mind prompts you to betray God. And you do it. You feel that God's fulfillment must come only through your fulfillment. If it does not work out that way, you are not prepared to sacrifice one iota of your life-breath to fulfill God here on earth. Your divine promise sheds bitter tears of failure. Needless to say, to try to fulfill yourself before you have fulfilled God is to put the cart before the horse. It is the height of absurdity.

Perhaps by now you have come to learn what has made you fail in your most sincere promise to God. It is your fear. If I ask you how many enemies you have, you will jump up and say, "Quite a few." But I have to say you are mistaken. You have just one enemy and that is all, even though, to your wide surprise, it seems like a host in itself. That single enemy of yours is fear, your unconsciously cherished fear.

You are afraid of the inner life. You feel that the moment you launch into the inner life you are lost, completely lost, like a babe in the woods. You may also think that in accepting the inner life, you are building castles in the air. Finally, you may feel that to accept the inner life is to throw your most precious life into the roaring mouth of a lion who will completely devour you and your outer life.

You have countless sweet dreams. You want to transform them into reality. All your dreams want to enjoy the world. You want to offer your momentous mite to the world at large; but you feel that if you embark on the inner life, you will be deprived of all these invaluable achievements. So now it is time for fear to make its appearance, and naturally you start shying away from the inner life. Fear starts torturing you. It tries to limit and bind you.

Unfortunately, your life yields to this deplorable mistake. But if once, only once, with the help of your all-energizing meditation, you could carry your long-cherished fear into the inner world, you would see that fear loses its very existence there. In the twinkling of an eye, it becomes one with the dynamic strength of your inner life.

If you want to truly possess the outer world, you have to possess the inner world first. Not the other way around. If you want to truly enjoy the outer world, you must enjoy the inner world first. Not vice versa. If your heart pines to serve humanity, you have to serve the inner divinity first. Infallible is this truth.

I FEAR

I fear to speak, I fear to speak.
My tongue is killed, my heart is weak.
I fear to think, I fear to think.
My mind is wild, and apt to sink.
I fear to see, I fear to see.
I eat the fruits of Ignorance-tree.
I fear to love, I fear to love.
A train of doubts around, above.
I fear to be, I fear to be.
Long dead my life of faith in me.

NO LITTLE ENEMY

There is no little enemy.
A wee fear
    Tortures our whole existence.
A tiny doubt
    Devours our entire being.
A puny jealousy
    Destroys our universal oneness.

KNOW THYSELF

University of Puerto Rico, Rio Piedras, Puerto Rico

August 26, 1968

Atmanam viddhi—Know thyself. Each individual has to know himself. He has to know himself as the infinite, eternal and immortal Consciousness. The concept of Infinity, Eternity and Immortality is absolutely foreign to us. Why? The reason is quite simple. We live in the body, rather than in the soul. To us the body is everything. There is nothing and can be nothing beyond the body. The existence of the soul we consider sheer imagination. But I assure you that the soul is not imaginary. It is at once the life and the revelation of the Cosmic Reality. Most of us live in the body, in the earthbound physical consciousness. Our teacher is Darkness; our professor is Ignorance. But if ever we live in the soul, we shall see that our teacher is Vision and our professor is Illumination.

"Life is effort." So says the body. "Life is blessing." So says the soul. The human in man does not want to go beyond morality, society and humanity. The divine in man comes down from divinity into humanity, from unity into multiplicity.

Atmanam viddhi. Know thyself. The seers of the Upanishads not only discovered this Truth Transcendental but offered it to the suffering, crying and striving mankind. In order to know oneself, one has to discover oneself first. What is self-discovery? Self-discovery is God-Realization.

Without Yoga there is no self-discovery. Yoga is not a religion. Yoga is the Universal Truth. It is the traditional truth of India. It is the most important experience of life. True Yoga and life go together. They cannot be separated. If you try to separate them, you will fail. Yoga and life are as inseparable as the Creator and the Creation.

Is Yoga another name for severe asceticism? Positively not. Is Yoga another name for self-discipline? Decisively yes. Does Yoga demand

22

the rejection of the world and the starvation of the senses? No, never. Does Yoga demand the acceptance of the world and mastery over the senses? Yes, a mighty Yes. Is Yoga for everybody? Yes and no. Yes, because each human soul has come from God and inwardly aspires to return to Him. No, because some people, at their present stage of development, feel they can live without God.

Can learning and reasoning offer man self-realization? No. Mere book knowledge ends in self-deception. Why? Because a man of knowledge feels that he has achieved the infinite wisdom. Unfortunately, he does not know that the real Infinite Wisdom can come only from God, from God-Realization. Mere mental reasoning ends in self-frustration.

Can dedication and aspiration offer man self-realization? Yes. Man's dedication is his heart-flower offered at the Feet of God. Man's aspiration is his soul-fruit placed in the Lap of God.

For self-realization, man needs freedom. God gives him freedom. What is freedom? Freedom is God's sacrifice-power and man's miracle-power. Sri Ramakrishna, the great spiritual Master of India, once remarked, "The wretch who constantly says, 'I am bound, I am bound,' only succeeds in being bound. He who says day and night, 'I am a sinner, I am a sinner,' verily becomes a sinner. One must have such burning faith in God that one can say, 'What? I have repeated God's name, so how can sin still cling to me? How can I be a sinner anymore?' "

We must cherish positive thoughts, positive ideas, positive ideals. Only then will our Goal no longer remain a far cry. Each man has to feel, "I am at the Feet of God, my own Master. I am in the Hands of God, my own Creator. I am in the Heart of God, my only Beloved."

"Ask and it shall be given to you; seek and ye shall find; knock and it shall be opened unto you." I asked. My Lord bestowed His boundless Compassion on me. I sought. My Lord gave me His infinite Love. I knocked. To my utter surprise, the door was not bolted from inside. My sweet Lord was eagerly expecting my arrival. Lo, I am come!

MY SELF-DISCOVERY

With a mere smile You cannot conquer my heart.
I want the most luminous discovery of my heart,
    along with Your Smile.
Those who want Your Smile can have the downpour
    of Your Infinite Smile in their hearts.
My self-awareness and my self-discovery alone can
    give me the flute of transformation.

THE SUPREME

Father, I have Seen.
        "No."
Father, I have Known.
        "No."
Father, I have Felt.
        "No."
Father, I have Become.
        "No."
Father, I AM.
        "Yes."

THE MEANING OF LIFE

Inter-American University, San Juan, Puerto Rico
October 17, 1968

Life is God's Transcendental Blessing to His Creation. What is more important than God's Blessing? God's Concern. What is more important than God's Concern? The absolute Fulfillment of God's Will.

Life is man's experience of wisdom and faith. Wisdom without faith is the bondage of futility. Faith without wisdom is the smile of stupidity. Faith and wisdom can go together. Faith awakens us to see the Truth. Wisdom helps us to live the Truth.

The outer world is a play of conflict between the fleeting and destructive thoughts of man's mind and the constructive and lasting will of man's soul. The inner world is a play of harmony between the mind's surrender and the soul's acceptance.

Life is will. There is only one will that mediates between God and man. That will is at once the descending cry of concern and compassion and the ascending cry of love and helplessness.

Life is man's conscious attempt to see God face to face.

> First try. Then cry. If necessary.
> First give. Then take. If necessary.
> First run. Then stop. If necessary.
> First be the doer. Then be the talker. If necessary.

Thought, human thought, rules the world. But mere thinking is of no avail.

> When I think, God is my frustration.
> When I cry, God is my consolation.
> When I try, God is my salvation.
> When I will, God is my illumination.

We must love God first if we really love life, for God is not only the Source but the very Breath of life. Love of God costs nothing, absolutely nothing, but is worth much. Our mind knows this truth. Our heart practices this truth. Our soul embodies this truth.

The ultimate aim of the human life is liberation. Liberation is the choice of man and the Grace of God. Liberation is man's total freedom and God's constant responsibility.

You cry because you have no plans to make your life meaningful and successful. He cries because all his plans have come to a lame conclusion. I cry because I do not want to have any plans. What I want is to be seated all the time at the Feet of the Supreme, who is at once the Vision and the Reality.

My life has three doctors: Dr. Love, Dr. Devotion and Dr. Surrender. Dr. Love cures my mind's narrowness. Dr. Devotion cures my heart's impurity. Dr. Surrender cures my life's ignorance.

My life has three Gods: God the Existence, God the Consciousness and God the Bliss. God the Existence eternally lives in me. God the Consciousness constantly grows in me. God the Bliss immortally lives with me.

A LIFE OF JOY

A life of joy is the love of God
And God's concern is a life of love
And life in love and love in life
Man's Perfection-Dawn below, above.

MY LIFE BEGAN

My life began with duty's pride,
My life shall live with beauty's light.
My life shall sport with reality's soul,
My life shall end with Divinity's Height.

MAN AND HIS GOAL

State University of New York at Farmingdale
December 11, 1968

My dear friends, you are fortunate, you are special.

A significant branch of the State University helps you to specialize here in horticulture and agriculture. Soon you are going to be at home in the science of plant life and soil cultivation. In a broader and purer sense, you are making a solemn promise to the world at large that you wish to be true children of Nature and Mother Earth.

I am sure you all know that it was an Indian scientist, Sir J. C. Bose, who discovered life in plants. He was born in Bengal. I am proud that I was born in the same province.

Your genuine love of nature enables and entitles you to receive special love, concern, favor and blessings from the Universe, the Universal Life and the Universal Mother.

> A man said to the universe, "Sir, I exist!"
> "However," replied the universe, "the fact has not created in me a sense of obligation."

Though it may be true for others, this striking pronouncement of Stephen Crane's does not apply to you in the least. I wish to tell you that the Universe, the Universal Life and the Universal Mother will proudly bless your devoted heads and dedicated hearts, for you love Nature, you adore Nature. What is Nature? Nature is God the Mother. In His masculine aspect, God is Transcendental. In His feminine aspect, God is Universal. Let us invoke the presence of God the Universal Mother before we enter into "Man and His Goal."

Man's false goal is human love. Human love sadly fails. Man's false goal is physical beauty. Physical beauty is only skin deep. Man's false goal is money and material wealth. "It is easier for a camel to pass through the eye of a needle than for a rich man to enter into the kingdom of Heaven."

27

Man's real goal is Truth. Truth awakens him from his ignorance-sleep. Man's real goal is Peace. Peace feeds him, his life inner and outer. Man's real goal is Bliss. Bliss immortalizes him, his life-breath.

Self-realization: this is what man needs from God. Love: this is what God needs from man. Faith: this is what God always has in man. But, alas, man has yet to develop faith in himself and faith in God.

Man unfalteringly says, "If I had time, I would love God. If I had time, I would worship God. If I had time, I would even cry for God."

But poor God has time. He has time to forgive man's unending stupidity. He has time to bless man's shameless mind and grant him all his real necessities. He has time even to cry for man's still unborn sincerity.

Man and God. Try to realize God. Both God and man will say to you, "Wonderful, go ahead." Try to explain God. Man will immediately tell you, "Stop. Don't belittle God, don't torture God." God will voice forth, "Stop. For My sake at least, don't deceive men, don't deceive My children."

Let us not try to explain God. If we do that, our ignorance will be exposed. Let all of us strive to realize God. For that, what we need is meditation. Let us meditate, meditate on God.

Man has to walk far, very far. He has to reach the Shores of the Golden Beyond. Slowly, steadily and unerringly he has to walk. But he must walk forward, not backward. Lincoln welcomes man, his fellow traveler, to sing with him, "I am a slow walker, but I never walk backward."

We believe in evolution. Man is not going back to the animal kingdom. Man is proceeding toward the kingdom of heaven, which perpetually breathes, grows and glows in the inmost recesses of his heart.

Friends, you are cultivating knowledge. We all do it. Each human being must own a bumper crop of knowledge.

Somebody said, "A college degree is often the receipt a young man gets for bills his father paid."

I will be bold enough to say that I reject this eyeless idea outright. Your parents want you to learn how to swim in the sea of knowledge. Your professors, who are expert swimmers in the sea of knowledge, teach you successfully and gloriously how to swim. I deeply admire your zealous sincerity and your professors' enormous capacity. But, alas, knowledge, book knowledge, is not enough. You all know it. I have not discovered something new or fantastic. Far from it. I am just reminding you of the soulful fact that there is another sea. This Sea is the Sea of Divine Light, Peace, Bliss and Power. This Sea gives you realization and liberation. You will have the realization of your conscious and indivisible oneness with God. You will have liberation from your bondage of millenia. This Sea gives you Fulfillment Infinite. Something more: this Sea makes you feel in a perfectly convincing manner that you are truly and unmistakably the God of tomorrow.

Who says that man is sleeping? This is not true. Man woke up with his teeming desires, but he was shamefully early. He discovered that God was not ready and would never be ready to receive him.

Man woke up with his flaming aspiration, but he was unpardonably late. Yet God was eager to receive him, embrace him and finally place him on His own Transcendental Throne.

ANOTHER DAY

Another day, another day.
My Lord Supreme is far away.

Another day, my heart can be
The all-giving breath of patience-tree.

Another day, my life can feed
My soulful world with its crying need.

Another day, I own to hear
God's Voice of Light and feel Him near.

Another day, another day.
My tears shall win His blue-gold Ray.

Another day, another day.
And then, no more my ignorance-clay.

Another day, I'll be God's Love
Within, without, below, above.

HOW TO LIVE IN TWO WORLDS

Sarah Lawrence College, Bronxville, N.Y.
January 14, 1969

> If I can stop one heart from breaking,
>   I shall not live in vain;
> If I can ease one life the aching,
>   Or cool one pain,
> Or help one fainting robin
>   Unto his nest again,
> I shall not live in vain.
>   —Emily Dickinson

My dear sisters:

I have come here to serve you. Serve I must. If I can serve even one amongst you in her endeavor toward self-discovery, I shall not have lived in vain. Nay, my life on earth will have found its purposeful meaning. You have every right to be proud of being devoted students at this college unparalleled in the United States. And today God presents me with a matchless opportunity to discover in you an aspiring heart.

Sarah Lawrence College is for women, as we all know. I wish to say a few words about Hindu women. I come from India, and I am sure you know by this time that I am a Hindu. A Hindu woman is the living embodiment of sanctity, devotion and faith. Purity is the hyphen between her life and her deeds. Intellectual education she does not care for. Her heart cries for the inner education, the education of the soul. This is no hyperbole. Her life of spontaneous and unending sacrifice is the soul of the Hindu race. In the hoary past, it was a Hindu woman, Maitreyi, who said to her husband, Yagnyavalkya, the peerless sage of the Upanishads, that nothing would satisfy her save Immortality.

When she said Immortality, she did not mean the prolongation of her physical existence for millions of years. She meant that she wanted to have the immortal consciousness, the consciousness of Immortality, within and without.

"After thirty years of research into the feminine soul, the great question which I haven't been able to answer is: what does a woman want?"—Freud. On behalf of women all over the world, Maitreyi's soul tells us what a woman wants.

There are two worlds: one is the world of Truth, the other is the world of Falsehood. What will decide when Truth and Falsehood disagree? Acceptance, their mutual acceptance. Truth will accept Falsehood to transform the life of Falsehood. Falsehood will accept Truth to manifest the breath of Truth.

Two worlds: one is known as Acceptance, the other as Rejection. I accept. I accept with my deepest gratitude what God has for me: Illumination. I reject with adamantine determination what the world has for me: Frustration.

Two worlds: Condition and Situation. Condition says, "God gives when you give." Situation says, "You are helpless. God alone can give and does give."

Unlike others, my God has two names: Delight and Compassion. In the inner world, I call Him by the name Delight. In the outer world, I call Him by the name Compassion. My God has two souls. The soul that He has in the inner world embodies His Dream. The soul that He has in the outer world reveals His Reality. My God has two bodies. His outer body is my Inspiration. His inner body is my Emancipation.

Heaven and hell represent two worlds in our consciousness. Heaven surprises hell with its boundless Joy. Hell surprises heaven with its ceaseless cry. Heaven says to hell, "I know how to dance and I can teach you if you want." Hell says to heaven, "Wonderful, you know how to dance and you are ready to teach me how to dance. But I wish to tell you that I know how to break my legs and I can break your legs too, if I want to."

Science and Spirituality are two different worlds. Science wants to shorten distances. Spirituality wants to unite distances. For me neither is enough. My vision wants to divinize and transform distance.

East and West: two worlds. We must unite them.

The awakened consciousness of man is visibly tending toward the Divine. This is a most hopeful streak of light amidst the surrounding obscurities of today. This is a moment, not merely of joining hands, but of joining minds, hearts and souls. Across all physical and mental barriers between East and West, high above national standards and individual standards, will fly the supreme banner of Divine Oneness.

The outer world is a world of reasoning mind. The inner world is a world of experience. The outer world finds it hard to believe in the existence of God. But in the inner world the existence of God always looms large. Sri Aurobindo said, "They proved to me by convincing reasons that God does not exist, and I believed them. Afterward I saw God, for He came and embraced me. And now which am I to believe, the reasoning of others or my own experience?"

Can we live in two worlds? Certainly we can. If we have spontaneous inspiration we can successfully live in the outer world and achieve our outer goals. If we have soulful aspiration we can live in the inner world and achieve our inner Goal. The outer world is the body. The inner world is the soul.

If we stay in the body, then we constantly have to abide by the dictates of the soul so that the body, instead of being a blind tool of fate, becomes a perfect channel for the Supreme, for His divine Manifestation in the physical. And if we want to live in the soul, to experience infinite Light, Peace and Bliss, then we must not neglect the body, we must not destroy the body, for it is inside the body that the soul abides on earth.

GOD AND THE WORLD

The world and God.
How to harmonize?
Difficult? No.
No wide surprise.
Our Father is God,
The world our Mother.
This living truth,
Our protecting cover.
Father is the Face,
Mother the Smile.
Without the one,
The other futile.

ONE MAN AND ONE WOMAN
CAN SAVE THE WORLD

One man can save the world.
Who is that man?
    That man is the man of Compassion.
One woman can save the world.
Who is that woman?
    That woman is the woman of Perfection.
Where does the man
Of Compassion live?
He lives in the Abode
    Of God's Transcendental Pride.
Where does the woman
Of Perfection live?
She lives in the Abode
    Of God's Eternal Gratitude.

DUTY SUPREME

Boston University, Boston, Mass.
March 24, 1969

The poet sang:

> I slept and dreamed that life was Beauty.
> I woke and found that life was Duty.

Duty and Beauty are like the North Pole and the South Pole.

What is Beauty? Beauty is the oneness of the finite and the Infinite. Beauty is the expression of the Infinite through man the finite. Beauty is man's embodiment of God, the Infinite. In the material world, in the physical world, it is through Beauty that God reveals Himself.

The Beauty of the soul is Beauty unparalleled in the physical world. This Beauty inspires the outer world and fulfills the inner world. This Beauty makes us one with God's Soul, the Light Infinite. This Beauty makes us one with God's Body, the Universe. When we live in the world of aspiration, we come to realize that the transcendental Duty and the universal Beauty are the perfect expressions of one and the same Reality.

Duty. In our day-to-day life, duty is something unpleasant, demanding and discouraging. When we are reminded of our duty, we lose all our inner, spontaneous joy. We feel miserable. We feel that we could have used our life-energy for a better purpose. Only a man devoid of common sense can say he does not know what his duty is. Each man knows his duty well, too well. It is up to him whether or not to perform it.

Today I am supposed to speak on Duty Supreme. An aspirant's is the life that has to perform the Duty Supreme. His first and foremost Duty is to realize God. There can be no other Duty except this Duty, God-Realization, in his life here on earth. An aspirant, when he saw the light of day, was inspired by God Himself with this message:

Realize Me on earth.
Reveal Me on earth.
Fulfill Me on earth.

Time is fleeting. Time does not wait for us. We shall have to be wise. We can utilize each moment for a divine purpose. We can utilize each moment in performing our soulful Duty.

Duty is painful, tedious and monotonous simply because we do it with our ego, pride and vanity. Duty is pleasant, encouraging and inspiring when we do it for God's sake. What we need is to change our attitude toward Duty. If we work for the sake of God, then there is no Duty. All is Joy. All is Beauty. Each action has to be performed and offered at the Feet of God. Duty for God's sake is the Duty Supreme. No right have we to undertake any other duty before we work out our own spiritual salvation. Did God not entrust us with this wonderful task at the time of our very birth? The Supreme Duty is to constantly strive for God-Realization. Time is short, but our souls' mission on earth is lofty. How can we waste time? Why should we spend time in the pleasures of the senses?

Now, we often say that we are under no obligation to others because we have not accepted anything from them. They have not given us anything. True, we are under no obligation, but there is a word called *expectation*. I may not have taken anything from you, but that does not mean that you cannot expect anything from me. At times your expectation may be legitimate. Expect you certainly can; but there is one thing that you cannot do. You cannot claim. You can expect, and it is up to me to give you what you want; but claim you must not. Only God can claim. God and God alone can claim from me my entire life. Each individual has to feel that God has the absolute right to claim him forever here on earth and there in heaven.

Love your family much. This is your great duty. Love mankind more. This is your greater duty. Love God most. This is your greatest duty, the Duty Supreme.

There are two things: one is remembrance, the other is forgetfulness. All of us know that it is our duty to collect our salary. Indeed, it is our duty. And we always remember it. But there is another duty. We have to work. That duty we forget. In order to get our salary, we have to work. Somehow we manage to forget this. In the spiritual world also, there is a duty. This duty is to enjoy the fruit of God-Realization. We all know it and we are extremely eager to perform this duty. But unfortunately we forget the other duty: meditation. One duty is to enjoy the fruits; the other duty is to acquire the fruits.

But we are clever enough to cry for the fruits of realization long before we have entered into the field of meditation. No meditation, no realization. Without meditation, God-Realization is nothing but self-deception.

An aspirant has a most significant duty, and that duty is to have perfect faith in his divine possibilities. If he has faith in himself and faith in the living Guru, then he can easily perform the Supreme Duty, the duty of Self-discovery, God-Realization.

I DO MY DUTY

I do my duty
    And
Let God's Compassion do the rest.
I do my duty
    And
Let God's Blessing do the rest.
I do my duty
    And
Let God's Assurance do the rest.
I do my duty
    And
Let God's Will do the rest.
I do my duty
    And
Let God's Pride do the rest.
I do my duty
    And
Let God's Oneness do the rest.

THE HERO MARCHES ALONG

He who loved this world
Has only got excruciating pangs.
The world has thrown on him
All ugliness, filth, dirt and impurity.
Yet the hero marches along
Carrying the burden of the entire world.
At the end of his teeming struggles
He will go and stand at the Feet of the Lord Supreme.

MY TASKS

I have only four tasks
    To perform:
Smile, fly, dive and run.
I have only three tasks
    To perform:
Smile, fly and dive.
I have only two tasks
    To perform:
Smile and fly.
I have only one task
    To perform:
Smile.

DO YOUR DUTY

Do your duty.
If you do your duty well,
    God will be proud of you.
    Do your duty.
If you succeed,
    Heaven will garland you.
    Do your duty.
If you fail,
    The world will embrace you.
Do your duty.
Do your duty,
    And thus
    Awaken your divinity.

GOD AND MYSELF

Brandeis University, Waltham, Mass.
March 26, 1969

Good evening. Sisters and brothers, let us know that good morning is God's morning, and good evening is God's evening. Good day is man's day, and good night is man's night. God's morning and evening say to man, "We do nothing but think of you." Man's day and night say to God, "We can do nothing but pray to you."

God and myself. God is my Father. God is my Mother. This is what I know. Also, I always know what to do.

When I say I know what to do, I am afraid you will misunderstand me. There is every possibility that you will doubt my sincerity.

Let me try to defend myself. Let me tell you my inmost secret: "I know what to do, precisely because God does it for me." You may then ask me why God does everything for me and not for you. If such is the case, God is unmistakably partial. To be sure, God is not partial. He is anything but that.

I know what to do, for God does it for me. I know that I do nothing and can do nothing. God is the Doer. God is the Action. God is the Fruit thereof. My life is an Eternal Experience of God.

Unfortunately there is a slight difference between your approach to God and my approach to God. Do you remember what the Son of God said to humanity? He said, "I and my Father are one." I believe in the Son of God. I try to live this truth. I also believe in our Vedic seers of the hoary past. They said, *"Brahmasmi"*—"I am the Brahman. I am the One without a second." I also have implicit faith in Sri Krishna's teaching, which I have learned from his *Gita*, the Song Transcendental: "A man is made by his faith. Whatever his faith is, so is he."

I know that God can be seen. I know that God can be felt. I know that God can be realized. I know that each human being, with no exception, will grow into God's Transcendental Vision and His Reality Absolute.

You are apt to cherish a few striking ideas in the inmost recesses of your heart. First of all, you get joy in telling the world that there is no God. There can be no such thing as God. Even when you feel that there is a God, you tell your near and dear ones that God is for them and for others, but not for you. With all the ignorance at your command, you proclaim that God does not care for you. You feel that God is terribly angry with you, for ten years ago you told a fatal lie, or deceived someone in the street. Poor God, as if He has nothing else to do than to get angry with you and punish you mercilessly.

Believe it or not, I tell you that God has many, many significant things to do with your life. To you, your life is nothing, a perfect zero. To God, your life is everything—to be precise, His everything. You are His unparalleled Pride. You are His only Dream. You are His only Reality. With you He sings the Song of Immortality. In you He sees the embodiment of His Existence-Consciousness-Bliss. For you, only for you, He exists through Eternity. He molds you. He shapes you. He guides you. He transforms you into His very Image, His Life of the ever-transcending Beyond.

Dear students, dear professors, dear sisters and brothers, you are now in the same boat as I. Together let us sing: "I know what to do, for God does it for me."

Let me sing one more song. And I do hope that you all will learn it soon. This song tells me what to say and what to aspire for:

Lead me from the unreal to the Real.
Lead me from darkness to Light.
Lead me from death to Immortality.

GOD'S ABSENCE AND GOD'S PRESENCE

O Lord, Thy absence has measureless Power.
Pangs of bitter failures rage through my mind.
Hot knives stab through my heart with every breath.
I know, I know, I am the eternal blind.

O Lord, Thy Presence has fathomless Power.
Who says, my soul is limp with black despair?
Eternity sits at my feet like a slave,
And Death—a weeping child, helpless, bare.

ANOTHER GOD

If I could only love myself
    Divinely,
I would become
    Another God.
If I could only reveal myself
    Selflessly,
I would become
    Another God.
If I could only manifest myself
    Unconditionally,
I would become
    Another God.
If I could only forget and forgive myself,
I would become
The only God.

MY LIFE ALTERNATES WITH GOD

My day alternates with night
My fear alternates with strength
My doubt alternates with certainty
My love alternates with hatred
My defeat alternates with victory
I alternate with God
My soul alternates with God the Dream
My heart alternates with God the Lover
My life alternates with God the Player.

DESIRE AND ASPIRATION

New York University, New York, N.Y.
March 29, 1969

America's fond child is New York. New York's fond child is New York University. This evening I wish to offer my sincere affection, true admiration and humble dedication to you, O fond children of New York University.

Desire is a wildfire that burns and burns and finally consumes us. Aspiration is a glowing fire that secretly and sacredly uplifts our consciousness and finally liberates us.

Thirst for the Highest is aspiration. Thirst for the lowest is annihilation.

Desire is expectation. No expectation, no frustration. Desire killed, true happiness built. Aspiration is surrender, and surrender is man's conscious oneness with God's Will.

As war brings the commerce of a country to a standstill, even so our tremendous inclination toward the pleasures of ignorance brings all our inner spiritual movements to a standstill.

As things exist at present, our very birth compels us to be far away from God. Why wallow deliberately in the pleasures of the senses and move even farther away from God? Indeed, to satisfy the imagined necessities of our human life and cry for the fulfillment of our earthly pleasures can be nothing but self-torturing evil. But to satisfy God's necessities, real and divine, in us and through us, is self-illumination.

Poor God, unillumined men always take You amiss. They think that You are merciless. Yet when You fulfill their lecherous desires, they think that nobody on earth can surpass You in stupidity.

Now, poor man, look at your most deplorable fate. In the apt words of George Bernard Shaw, "There are two tragedies in life. One is not to get your heart's desire; the other is to get it."

Desire means anxiety. This anxiety finds satisfaction only when it is able to fulfill itself through solid attachment. Aspiration means calmness. This calmness finds satisfaction only when it is able to express itself through all-seeing and all-loving detachment. In desire and nowhere else abides human passion. Human passion has a dire foe called judgment, the judgment of the divine dispensation.

In aspiration and nowhere else dwells man's salvation. Man's salvation has an eternal friend called Grace, God's all-fulfilling Grace.

Desire is temptation. Temptation nourished, true happiness starved. Aspiration is the soul's awakening. The soul's awakening is the birth of supernal delight.

A true seeker of the infinite Truth can never gain anything from Oscar Wilde's discovery that "the only way to get rid of a temptation is to yield to it." The seeker has already discovered the truth that it is only through high, higher and highest aspiration that one can get rid of all temptations, seen and unseen, born and yet to be born.

Wilde says something else, and this is quite significant: "I can resist everything except temptation." Needless to say, nobody blames him for that, for temptation is a universal disease. For a man without aspiration, temptation is unmistakably irresistible. But a true seeker feels and knows that he can resist temptation and what he cannot resist is transformation, the transformation of his physical nature, his entire consciousness, in the bosom of the sea of Time. Of course, the transformation of his physical nature, his entire earthly consciousness, is something he never did and never will resist. On the contrary, it is for this transformation that he lives on earth.

Look at the strength of a bubble of desire! It has the power to encage our entire life for its use alone. Look at the strength of an iota of aspiration! It has the power to make us feel that God the Infinite is absolutely ours. And something more: that God's infinite Love, Peace, Joy and Power are for our constant use.

The objects of the senses and man's attachment to them are inseparable. But the moment they see the smile of God, they deny their intimacy. What is more, they become perfect strangers.

Fulfill your body's demands, and you lose your self-control. Fulfill your soul's needs, and you gain your self-control.

Don't embrace vice. In refraining, you will possess something more valuable: self-control. What is self-control? It is the power that tells you that you don't have to run toward your goal. The goal has to come to you, and it shall.

The capital of the outer world is money, which very often changes itself into poisonous honey. The capital of the inner world is aspiration, which eventually transforms itself into self-realization.

The acme of human desire is represented by Julius Caesar's *Veni, vidi, vici*—"I came, I saw, I conquered." The pinnacle of divine aspiration was voiced by the Son of God: "Father, let Thy Will be done."

Passion's slave is man. God's child is likewise man. Which do you want to be, God's child or passion's slave? Choose. One selection leads you to utter destruction, the other to immediate salvation. Choose; you are given the golden and unconditional choice. Choose; choose you must. Here and now.

DESIRE-SUN, ASPIRATION-MOON

Desire-Sun makes me tremble.
Aspiration-Moon makes me dream.
O Desire-Sun, in you
I have my silent death.
O Aspiration-Moon, with you
I have my endless Life.

HOW TO PLEASE GOD

University of Bridgeport, Bridgeport, Conn.

April 14, 1969

How to please God? I can please God by offering Him what I have and what I am. What I have is gratitude. What I am is aspiration. If I want to please Him more, then I must never consider my life a sad failure, but rather a constant experience of His. If I want to please Him most, not only in one but in every aspect of life, then I must feel that, unlike me, He sees my life, inner and outer, as the Song of His own Life-Breath, the Song of His perfection, growing into His own perfect Perfection Absolute.

Do you know when you hurt God? You hurt God the moment you underestimate your inner capacity. You hurt God the moment you exaggerate your self-imposed outer responsibility. You hurt Him deeply when you cherish the futile idea that God-Realization is not for you. To be sure, your God-Realization is the mightiest affirmation, the greatest certainty at God's choice Hour.

Unfortunately there are people in whose lives the very question of pleasing or hurting God does not arise at all. They do not believe God exists. True, they have not seen God, but that does not mean they are qualified to deny His existence. What about those who have seen Him, felt Him and realized Him, and are fulfilling Him in this world and other worlds? I tell the unbelievers and disbelievers that they are not only mercilessly deceiving themselves in the inner life of divinity, but also unendingly carrying themselves away, far away from the outer life of reality. There are people who deny the existence of God outright. The eager desire of Christ's disciple Thomas to have proof is found the world over: "Blessed are they that have not seen, and yet have believed." Let the message of the Son of God reverberate in the inmost recesses of each human heart, aspiring or unaspiring, inspired or uninspired. Today, faith is the harbinger of reality. Tomorrow, faith and reality will move together. The day after tomorrow, faith and reality will fulfill each other. Faith fulfills reality in its embodiment of reality. Reality fulfills faith by revealing itself through faith.

The feeling of gratitude makes a man truly happy, and God is pleased when a man is truly happy. Dostoevsky declares, "I believe the best definition of man is the ungrateful biped." This may be true when a man swims in the sea of his body's ignorance. But when a man lives and swims in the sea of his soul's light, he is all gratitude. He is the constant expression and spontaneous revelation of God the Receiver and God the Achiever.

According to Paul Valéry, "The soul is the wife of the body. They do not have the same kind of pleasure, or at least they seldom enjoy it at the same time." First of all, the spiritual world has already discovered for certain that the soul is neither masculine nor feminine. It is above and beyond these two dividing zones. Hence the soul can never be the wife of the body. The Upanishads have taught us that the body is the chariot and the soul is the master of the chariot. Valéry is absolutely right when he says that the body and the soul do not have the same kind of pleasure. We know that the body gets pleasure in ignorance and from ignorance. Slowly, gradually and unerringly we come to realize that the body's pleasure is ignorance itself. In the case of the soul, instead of using the word "pleasure" we should use the word "delight." The soul feels delight in and from Infinity and Eternity. The soul's delight is the flowing Infinity; the soul's delight is the glowing Eternity. When the aspirant's meditation transforms the desire-pleasure of the body into aspiration-delight, the soul and the body not only will eat the same food, but will eat it at the same time. And their food is Truth. Truth at once awakens the body and pilots the soul.

The other day somebody said to me that God is pleased with him all the time, for one secret reason. He then volunteered to tell me his precious secret: "Although I have many things to say against God's creation, even against God Himself, I just cleverly ignore His world of countless imperfections and mightily flatter Him in silence and in public. That is why God is so pleased with me all the time; and well He ought to be."

I said to him, "My dear friend, there is a slight difference between you and me. Your sense of imperfection in God's world is entirely different from mine. You feel that imperfection is something discouraging, disheartening, dirty and finally damaging. I take imperfection as something growing, something that has still to complete its journey. I take imperfection as an unavoidable rung in the ladder of gradual and ultimate perfection. I take imperfection as a significant experience God Himself is having in and through man's life. And this same God will enjoy perfection, perfect Perfection, in and through each individual in the bosom of Eternity. Now, as regards your flattery of God, God needs no human flattery. You don't have to flatter Him to gain His Love, Concern and Blessing. God neither expects nor demands flattery from you. God is not a beggar. He does not expect anything of you. God is not an autocrat. He does not demand anything from you. What God is, is Love. What God is, is Joy. If you can love yourself soulfully, if you can discover your true inner Joy, then you will see that God has already been pleased with you. Don't try to please God by deceiving Him. We can't deceive God. Never. We can't even deceive any human being on earth. At most what we can do and what we in fact do, is to deceive ourselves. Emerson is perfectly right when he affirms, 'It is impossible for a man to be cheated by anyone but himself.' "

To come back to our original question: how to please God? The easiest and most effective way to please God is by constant and unconditional self-offering. Let us try. We shall, without fail, succeed. Lo, God is standing right in front of us. He is pleased. God is really and truly pleased with us.

REVEALING SOUL AND
FULFILLING GOAL

If You but knew,
Father, what I have done for You.
Planted and raised a climbing tree
For You to dance on its top smiling free.

If You but knew,
Father, what I have done for You.
I have become the world's lowest slave
Your Breath to serve in man, the grave.

"If you but knew,
Child, what I ever think of you.
You are My Life's revealing Soul,
You are My Vision's fulfilling Goal."

THE SECRET OF INNER PEACE

University of Connecticut, Storrs, Conn.
April 19, 1969

Dear sisters and brothers, I shall show you how to acquire, here and now, inner peace. My help is not advice. Mine is not the way to advise people what to do or what not to do. It is true that everyone is unselfish and liberal when it comes to giving advice and, unfortunately, I am no exception. Yet I fully agree with Chesterfield, who says, "Advice is seldom welcome and those who need it the most, like it the least."

This world of ours has everything except one thing: peace. Everybody wants and needs peace, whether he be a child or an octogenarian. But the idea of peace is not the same for each individual. It sadly differs. A child's idea of peace is to beat a drum. Beating a drum brings him joy, and this joy is his peace. An old man's idea of peace is to sit quietly with his eyes and ears closed, so that he can escape the fond embrace of the ugly and restless world. The general in Eisenhower spoke on peace: "We are going to have peace, even if we have to fight for it."

The indomitable Napoleon voiced forth, "What a mess we are in now: peace has been declared." The Son of God taught us, "Blessed are the peacemakers, for they shall inherit the earth."

Somebody has very aptly said, "The more we strive for peace on earth, the more it seems that the dove of peace is a bird of paradise."

To be sure, peace is not the sole monopoly of heaven. Our earth is extremely fertile. Here on earth we can grow peace in measureless measure.

I am supposed to speak on the inner peace. I wish to confine my talk to the spiritual seeker in each of you. A genuine seeker after peace must needs be a seeker after love. Love has another name: sacrifice. When sacrifice is pure, love is sure. When love is divine, in sacrifice there can be no "mine," no "thine." Love is the secret of oneness. Sacrifice is the strength of oneness. Self-love is self-indulgence. Self-indulgence is self-annihilation. Love of God is the seeker's greatest opportunity to realize God.

We sacrifice our precious time to make money. We sacrifice our hard-earned money to fight against time. In order to have something from the outer world, we have to sacrifice something of our own. Similarly, in the inner world we offer our aspiration in return for God-Realization. The flame of our aspiration is kindled by God Himself. The fruit of our realization, too, we get from God directly. God is the Inspirer in us. God is the Eternal Giver. God is the Eternal Receiver in us. God uses aspiration to take us to Himself. God uses realization to bring Himself to us. God is sacrifice when we live in the world of aspiration. God is sacrifice when we live in the realm of realization. But God says that there is no such thing as sacrifice. There is only one thing here on earth and there in heaven, and that thing is called oneness: the fulfillment in oneness and the fulfillment of oneness.

There are four kinds of seekers: lamentable, incapable, promising and fulfilling. The lamentable and the incapable have to be patient; they have to wait for the Hour of God. The promising and the fulfilling are already singing and dancing in the Hour of God. They are constantly meditating on God. This is their inner life of realization. They are soulfully and spontaneously acting for God. This is their outer life of revelation.

To come back to the secret of inner peace, our questioning and doubting mind is always wanting in peace. Our loving and dedicated heart is always flooded with inner peace. If our mind has all the questions, then our heart has all the answers. The answers are perfect precisely because they come straight from the soul, which sees the Truth and lives in the Truth. And Truth, Truth alone, is the Goal of Goals.

If you want to have the inner peace, then you must follow the path of spirituality. Spirituality is the answer. There are three ages of man: under-age, over-age and average. To the under-age, spirituality is hocus-pocus. To the over-age, spirituality is something dry, uncertain and obscure. And to the average, spirituality is self-oblivion, self-negation and self-annihilation.

But a true seeker will say that spirituality is something normal, natural, spontaneous, fertile, clear, luminous, divinely self-conscious, self-affirmative and self-creating. If you have a spiritual teacher to help and guide you, then you are very lucky. Listen to him always, until you breathe your last. If you stop taking advice from him, then yours will be the loss and not his. Even in the ordinary human life one needs a teacher, a mentor. There is considerable truth in what Churchill says: "In those days he was wiser than he is now—he used, frequently, to take my advice."

If you don't have a spiritual Master and if you don't care for one, then at every moment please listen to the dictates of your soul in absolute silence. Peace you want and need. To have peace, you must have free access to your soul. To have free access to your soul, you must have inner silence. To have inner silence, you need aspiration. To have aspiration, you need God's Grace. To have God's Grace, you must feel that you are God's and God's alone, always!

We are now in Connecticut. The motto of Connecticut is supremely significant. My heart of devotion and my soul of love are singing the matchless motto of Connecticut: *Qui Transtulit Sustinet* —"He who transplanted sustains." God transplanted truth to earth, and He sustains this truth with love. In the combination of the two lies the secret of inner peace.

WHERE IS THE TRUTH?

O Lord, where is the Truth?
    "Where your Beloved is."
Who is my Beloved, who?
    "In Whom your life is peace."

DO YOU NEED?

Do you need peace of mind?
Then think that the world does not need you.
Do you need peace of mind?
Then feel that the world
Is not nearly as useless as you think.
Do you need peace of mind?
Then see that you do not make
The same mistakes
That the world quite often makes.

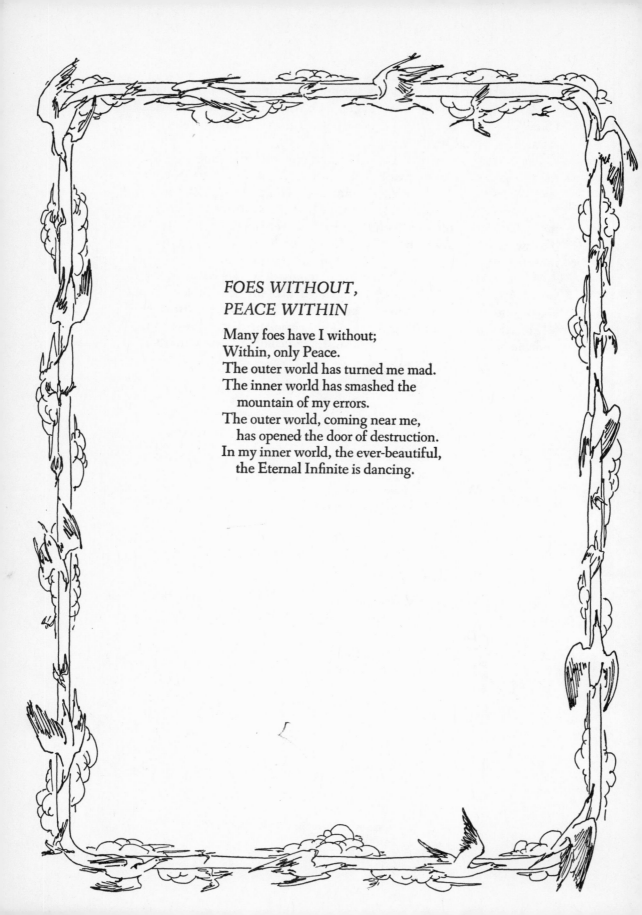

FOES WITHOUT,
PEACE WITHIN

Many foes have I without;
Within, only Peace.
The outer world has turned me mad.
The inner world has smashed the
    mountain of my errors.
The outer world, coming near me,
    has opened the door of destruction.
In my inner world, the ever-beautiful,
    the Eternal Infinite is dancing.

THE QUINTESSENCE OF MYSTICISM

American University, Washington, D.C.
April 21, 1969

There are three principal paths that lead to God-Realization: the path of Selfless Service, the path of Love and Devotion and the path of Knowledge and Wisdom. Raja Yoga (Mysticism) is a significant aspect of the Yoga of Knowledge (Jnana Yoga). The Knowledge Supreme is something infinitely more than mere philosophical knowledge. Mysticism is experience, the direct and intimate experience of Truth. After covering a great distance in the path of knowledge, philosophy gets tired and takes rest. Mysticism begins when and where philosophy ends. The seers, after having personally experienced the knowledge of Truth, revealed it to the world at large.

The seers sing:

> Him I have known, the Being Supreme,
> Refulgent, luminous as the Sun beyond darkness,
> Far beyond the embrace of devouring gloom.

The seers teach us that the Transcendental Reality and the All-Embodying Existence are one and the same.

A mystic takes unity and diversity as one. Further, he sees unity in diversity. He tells the world that the One and the Many are one. The One is Many in its universal form. The Many are One in their transcendental form. In our spiritual life, we come across two significant words: *occultism* and *mysticism.* Occultism is secrecy and cries for secrecy. It wants to house everything in top secrecy. Mysticism is not like that. Mysticism is ready to offer its achievement, transcendental Knowledge, to all who cry for it.

The difference between a philosopher and a mystic lies in the fact that a philosopher, with the greatest difficulty, sees from a distance, and rather imperfectly, the body of Truth, whereas a mystic enters into the very soul of Truth at his sweet will and can live there as long as he wants. And, also, he is permitted by the Supreme to bring to the fore the vast wealth of the soul and share it with the seekers of Truth. Mysticism affirms that the Knowledge of the Divine is universal.

Let us for a moment enter into the lore of the supernal mystery of the *Vak* in the Vedas. *Vak* is The Word. *Vak* at once embodies and reveals the Truth. In its embodiment of Truth, it receives creative inspiration in infinite measure from the Supreme. In its revelation of Truth, it offers to mankind the Supreme, the Liberator Supreme. *Vak* is the connecting link between two worlds: the world that has not yet realized and fulfilled itself and the world that has already realized and is fulfilling itself.

Mysticism has a language of its own. Its name is Intuition. In it, no mind or mental analysis can ever exist. A mystic sits on the wings of the Intuition-Bird and flies to the Ultimate Real. Intuition reveals the perfect oneness of the Transcendental Vision and Absolute Reality. A mystic is sincere enough to tell the Truth. He says that it is next to impossible for him to interpret his inner experience. No word or thought can do justice to his experience. At this point the Vedic seer cries out, "What shall I speak, what verily shall I think?" The poor mind and senses are no longer alive, having collapsed in their race toward the Unknown. Not for them the Ultimate Mystery of the Universe. Not for them the Knowledge of the Beyond. Mysticism emphasizes the unity of all souls in the Universal Soul. When we look at the Universe, we see it as the scene of conflict between good and evil, darkness and light, ignorance and knowledge. Needless to say, this struggle commenced long before the appearance of man and still continues. The light works in and through the aspiring soul; the darkness works in and through the unaspiring soul. The real transformation of human nature comes not through an austere, ascetic life or a complete withdrawal from the world, but through a gradual and total Illumination of life. And for that, one needs aspiration. Aspiration, and aspiration alone, is the precursor of this Illumination.

A mystical experience is the aspirant's inner certitude of Truth. This certitude rests on revelation. Revelation is inner authority. Inner authority is final. And who has this authority? Not he who is a victim of merciless logic, but he who has had the experience and who has now grown into the experience itself. Logic is the reasoning and reasoned truth, which is the pride of the finite. Mysticism is the revealing and revealed Truth, which is the pride of the Infinite. If we believe in mysticism, then we must realize that the Ultimate Truth is not only above reason, but contrary to reason. If we believe something through reason, we enter onto the life-torturing path of plurality, the unconscious plurality of separateness. But when we believe something through our inner, mystic faith, we enter onto the life-giving and life-fulfilling path of unity's Transcendental Reality.

Martin Luther vehemently distrusted the effectiveness of reason. Nor did he have any faith in ritual or in mere work as a means to salvation. In his mysticism, we see the smiling and convincing face of faith. Faith alone can bring about salvation. Faith alone has the key to salvation.

Existence and essence live together. They are one. In the thirteenth century, Meister Johannes Eckhart dynamically asserted this view. We have to realize that essence is singularly manifest in the divine qualities of the human soul, whereas existence is gloriously manifest in the human qualities of the divine soul. The end of the journey for the human soul is complete union with God. The end of the journey for the divine soul is the absolute manifestation of God.

Mysticism tells us that God-Realization can be attained not by the practice of ideas, but by the constant feeling of oneness with Truth. An idea, at best, indicates the passive aspect of the sense-world because a mental formation is directly or indirectly caught by the sense-world. But the feeling of oneness with Truth easily transcends the sense-world and indicates and ascertains the active and dynamic aspect of life's evolving process in the flowing stream of Eternity.

A mystic tells the world that God's Body is Wisdom and God's Soul is Love. A worldly man feels that his body and his physical activities fashion his soul. A mystic smilingly says that it is the soul that molds the body and transforms it into the unlimited consciousness-light of the soul.

According to Santayana, "Mysticism is not a religion, but a religious disease." Santayana is perfectly right when he says that mysticism is not a religion. In my opinion, mysticism is the highest aspiration that religion embodies. But as for "religious disease," I can never agree with Santayana in his profound realization.

I want to say with all the spiritual confidence at my command that mysticism serves as a panacea; not only for those who cry to see their Beloved God's Face, but also for those who are afraid of seeing God's Face in His Omniscience and His Omnipotence; and even for those who are at once mercilessly and unpardonably unbelievers and disbelievers in the very existence of God.

THE ESSENCE

Desire is the essence
Of a desiring man.
Doubt is the essence
Of a blinding man.
Fear is the essence
Of a bound man.
Aspiration is the essence
Of an aspiring man.
Bliss is the essence
Of a serving man.
Surrender is the essence
Of a God-man.

ACTION AND LIBERATION

George Washington University, Washington, D.C.
April 22, 1969

George Washington, first to embody America's hope,
First in inspiration, first in confidence, first in war,
First in victory,
First in conquering the heart of his Nation,
First to envisage a federation of states,
Single, powerful, united, whole.

"Blessed is he who has found his work; let him ask no other blessedness."—Carlyle. A spiritual person has found his work. His work is
selfless service. His work is dedicated action. Indeed, he has no need
of any other blessedness. His action is the divine acceptance of earthly
existence. And for this he needs a perfect body, a strong mind, a
soulful heart and a supremely inspired life of inner receptivity and
outer capacity.

Action is entering into the battlefield of life. Action is conquering
life's untold miseries and teeming limitations. Action is transforming
life's devouring imperfection into glowing perfection. Action is something infinitely deeper and higher than the mere survival of physical
existence. Action is the secret supreme, which enables us to enter into
the Life Eternal.

He who has not consciously accepted the spiritual life may consider action a necessary evil and the mother of bitter frustration. But
to a spiritual person, action is a divine blessing. It is the matchless
victory over bondage and ignorance. It is at once God's soulful Vision
in heaven and God's fruitful Mission on earth. God says that a man of
divine action is the ideal hero. This ideal hero divine manifests God
here on earth. To him, God-Realization is not enough. His is the heart
that cries for God's all-fulfilling Manifestation.

An unaspiring person dies and his role is over. An aspiring person dies and his role just begins. A spiritual Master leaves his body, and his mission starts bearing fruit.

Man is blind. He does not know what to do. When he wants to do something, he does not know how to go about it; and so, instead of getting joy from work, he immediately enters into difficulty.

T. H. Huxley pointedly remarks, "A man's worst difficulties begin when he is able to do as he likes." But if a man listens to the dictates of his soul and is able to do what his soul wants him to do, then his life will be transformed into golden opportunities and the greatest success will knock at his heart's door.

There is a saying that "the thumb takes the responsibility; the index finger, the initiative." Similarly man's aspiration takes the initiative, but it is God's Concern that takes the responsibility.

And someone has said, "The idealist walks on tiptoe, the materialist on his heels." Similarly, the divine hero-worker walks on the fire of self-illumination; the worker undivine, unaspiring and uninspired, who is full of ego, vanity and pride, walks on the fire of self-destruction.

According to some people, human life is just a cruel, meaningless and hopeless four-letter word: *work*. I wish to say they are mistaken. They like work; what they hate is the sense of labor, the burden of labor. *Labor* and *favor* perfectly rhyme. After all, whose favor is it? God's favor. Indeed, he is God's chosen child, and he alone is God's favorite, who works to please God. And in pleasing God, he realizes and fulfills himself. Then he tells the world that human life is a divinely meaningful three-letter word: *joy*.

Liberation. Liberation speaks: "We are not nature's slaves." Liberation teaches. It teaches us that our every heartbeat offers us a unique opportunity to achieve liberation. Liberation sings within us: "Arise, awake. Yours is the ideal Goal, the Goal of Goals."

Liberation is man's practical wisdom. Liberation is not a compromise with the world. Liberation is the end of man's competition with nature's temptation. Liberation elevates the earth-consciousness into the skies of the Beyond.

Which is more difficult: to cry for liberation or, after having been liberated, to cry for the illumination and transformation of the ignorance-loving, darkness-embracing world? Undoubtedly, the latter.

The poor liberated man: strange indeed is his fate. He constantly thinks of those who hardly ever think of him. When he stands before the world, the world acts like either a frightened child or a hostile child. A liberated man tells the world that God is not only knowable, but more than knowable. He also tells the world that it is easier to know God than to know the world, because when he wants to know the world he has to know it through God and from God.

Sri Krishna is Illumination Incarnate. The Buddha is Liberation Incarnate. The Christ is Salvation Incarnate.

The world is offering its Darkness to Sri Krishna. The world is offering its Suffering to the Buddha. The world is offering its Sin to the Christ.

The fallen consciousness of the world is flying toward the Highest Beyond to be touched by Christ, the Savior. The broken consciousness of the world is diving into the Deepest Beyond to be embraced by Buddha, the Liberator. The molten consciousness of the world is marching toward the Farthest Beyond to be blessed by Krishna, the Illuminator.

DO NOT CONVERT
AND DO NOT BE CONVERTED

Do not convert.
Let him go in his own way.
Do not be converted.
You must go in your own way.
Do not convert.
His resistance-night
Will devour your inner joy.
Do not be converted.
Your resistance-night
Will devour his inner joy.
God will ask His Freedom
To love you.
God will ask your freedom
To feed Him.
Do not convert,
Do not be converted.

THE STORY OF A SAINT

Is he a saint?
    Catch him,
    Strike him,
    Kill him,
Since he is not
    Adding anything
To our world's
    Practical and real life.
Ah, he is gone!
    He is dead!
His silent gaze
        We miss so deeply.
His pure life
        We miss so badly.
His heart of compassion
        We miss so sadly.
His soul of illumination
        We miss so unmistakably.
Alas, he is gone!
    No more our saint is with us.

THE SUPREME SECRET OF MEDITATION

University of Maryland, College Park, Md.
April 23, 1969

Meditation is man's thirst for the Infinite Real, Eternal Real and Absolute Real. The secret of meditation is to achieve conscious and constant oneness with God. The secret supreme of meditation is to feel God as one's very own, and finally to realize God for God's sake, Him to reveal and Him to fulfill.

Meditation has to be practiced spontaneously, soulfully and correctly. If it is not, dark doubt will blight your mind and utter frustration will steal into your heart. And you will probably find your whole existence thrown into the depths of a yawning chasm.

For meditation you need inspiration. Scriptures can supply you with inspiration. To buy a spiritual book takes ten seconds. To read that book takes a few hours. To absorb that book takes a few years. And to live the truths thereof may take not only a whole lifetime, but a few incarnations.

For meditation you need aspiration. The presence, physical or spiritual, of a spiritual teacher can awaken your sleeping aspiration. He can awaken your sleeping aspiration. He can easily and will gladly do it for you. Aspiration: this is precisely what you need in order to reach your journey's goal. You don't have to worry about your realization. Your aspiration will take care of it.

Meditation nourishes your self-discipline. Self-discipline strengthens your meditation. Meditation purifies your heart. And in a pure heart alone looms large the Godward march of human life. One may know what proper meditation is. One may even practice it, since that is what the divine nature in man needs. But the result or fulfillment of meditation transcends all human understanding, for it is measureless, limitless, infinite.

Meditation tells you only one thing: God *is*. Meditation reveals to you only one truth: yours is the vision of God.

To my extreme sorrow, some of you in the West have grave misconceptions about meditation. You feel that the acme of meditation is fortunetelling or miracle-mongering. *Fortunetelling* does not rhyme with *meditation*. *Miracle-mongering* does not rhyme with *meditation*, either. But *realization* perfectly rhymes with *meditation*. *Liberation* soulfully rhymes with *meditation*. Do you really want to realize God? Do you really want God's Infinite Light, Peace and Bliss? If so, you should keep millions and millions of miles away from fortunetellers and miracle-mongers. If you think that they inspire you, then you are mistaken. Go deep within and you will discover that they have just aroused your idle, eyeless and fruitless curiosity. Curiosity is not spirituality. And secretly and consciously the fortunetellers and miracle-mongers have offered you something more: temptation. Temptation is the harbinger of destruction. It is here that the divine mission of your life—unsuccessful, unfulfilled—comes to an end. Let us be on the alert. I urge you not to confuse your heart's genuine meditation with fortunetelling and miracle-mongering. Don't waste your time. Your time is precious. Your meditation is priceless. Your achievement shall be the treasure of timeless Eternity, measureless Infinity and deathless Immortality. Don't wait. All things come to him who waits, except the realization that "today" embodies and the liberation that "now" reveals.

Meditation is our soul's cry for our life's perfect perfection. Perfection has not yet dawned on earth, but one day it will. Perfection is the ideal of human life. To quote Swami Vivekananda: "None of us has yet seen an ideal human being, and yet we are told to believe in him. None of us has yet seen an ideally perfect man, and yet without that ideal we cannot progress."

Meditation alone can give birth to perfection. Meditation carries us beyond the frustration of the senses, beyond the limitation of the reasoning mind. And, finally, meditation can present us with the breath of perfection.

The ultimate aim of meditation is to realize the Supreme. The Katha Upanishad has a spiritual message to offer to the world. This message is an inner message.

> Higher than the senses are the objects of the senses.
> Higher than the objects of the senses is the mind.
> Higher than the mind is the intellect.
> Higher than the intellect is the Great Self.

Higher than the Great Self is the Unmanifest.
Higher than the Unmanifest is the Person.
Higher than the Person there is nothing at all.
That is the goal. That is the highest course.

Indeed, the Person is the Supreme Himself. On the strength of our highest and deepest meditation we unfailingly gain free access to the Supreme.

At the beginning of our spiritual journey, we feel that meditation is self-effort and perspiration. At the end of our journey's close, we realize that meditation is God's Grace, His Compassion Infinite.

The price is never right. Before realization, it is too high. After realization, it is too low.

HE RUNS THE FASTEST

He runs the fastest who does not run at all,
And who, like Lord Shiva, is in deep meditation, trancebound, still,
Day and night.
And those who run toward the oasis in the deserts of desire,
How can they search for the Light Supreme?

WHEN I PRAY,
WHEN I MEDITATE

When I pray
  God embraces
  My crying heart,
  My surrendering heart,
  My dreaming heart.
When I meditate
  God blesses my life,
  God caresses my soul,
  God reveals my Goal.

THE SAMADHIS

What is *savikalpa* samadhi?
Savikalpa samadhi
    Is
  The experience
Of Purity-sea
    And
Integrity-sky.

What is *nirvikalpa* samadhi?
Nirvikalpa samadhi
    Is
  The experience
Of loftiest
Self-transcendence.

What is *sahaja* samadhi?
Sahaja samadhi
    Is
Reality's message simplified:
Ignorance lost
  Forever
    And
Immortality won.

In the Cosmic Game
  You discover
That you eternally and supremely are
    What all along,
  From time immemorial,
You have been
Helplessly and desperately
  Aspiring to become.

WHEN

When he concentrates,
    Everything matters.
When he meditates,
    Nothing matters.
When he contemplates,
    Only God matters.

PRAYER

    Prayer
Is the youngest brother.
    He cries and cries
      To see Father's heights.
    Meditation
Is the eldest brother.
    He smiles and smiles
      To house Father's heights.
    Prayer
Tells me
    Where to go.
    Meditation
Tells me
  How to live.

THE SECRET SUPREME

University of North Dakota, Grand Forks, N.D.
May 6, 1969

The Secret Supreme is the Supreme Himself. He can be seen. He can be felt. He can be realized. When He is seen, He is Existence. When He is felt, He is Consciousness. When He is realized, He is Delight. In His embodiment of Existence, He is Eternal. In His revelation of Consciousness, He is Infinite. In His manifestation of Delight, He is Immortal. His Vision Transcendental and His Reality Absolute are man's future achievements. Man's expanding love, crying devotion and glowing surrender are God's future possessions.

God is at once finite and Infinite. He is in space. He can be measured. He must be measured. He is beyond space. He is measureless. He is boundless. He is Infinite. Smaller than the point of a needle is He. Larger than the seven higher worlds and seven lower worlds combined is He. In His Heart is earth's suffering. In His Soul is heaven's joy. Secretly He tells earth, "My child, I am yours. I am at your service. Use Me. Lo, you and I are fulfilled." Openly He tells heaven, "My child, you are Mine. You are at My service. Bend your head and go and give My Vision's Light and Reality's Height to your brother earth, younger in wisdom, older in patience."

The Secret Supreme is the Knowledge Supreme. This Knowledge is the song of liberation. This Knowledge is the dance of revelation. This Knowledge is the silence of perfection. When a man is liberated, he sits at the Feet of God. When a man reveals the highest Truth, he plays in the Heart of God. When a man is perfectly perfect, God will shake hands with him. Rest assured, one day God will send that perfect son of His into the world.

The world tells you a frightening secret: God is austere, God is demanding, God is stern. I tell you an illumining secret: God is reachable, God is lovable, God is enjoyable. When your mind is calm,

God is reachable. When your heart is pure, God is lovable. When your soul is sure, God is enjoyable.

For God's sake, do not be afraid of Him. He not only enjoys but appreciates your jokes. Your innocent jokes delight Him. The Vedic seer is now singing in you, through you and for you: "If, O God, Thou wert I, and I were Thee, Thy prayers should have their due fulfillment here and now."

And for your own sake, for your own joy and pride, you can sing along with the Vedic seers: "O God, Thee I shall not sell for the highest price, not for a thousand, not for ten thousand, not for an amount measureless, O my Lord Supreme of Infinity's Plenitude."

Self-realization is the Secret Supreme. Right now we are in both ignorance and knowledge. The Isha Upanishad teaches us that ignorance and knowledge should be pursued together. Through ignorance, we must conquer death. Through knowledge, we must obtain Immortality. Here ignorance means ritualistic actions, actions done for the sake of fruits. And knowledge means the deepest meditation that makes man consciously one with God; action done to fulfill God here on earth, there in heaven; truth for truth's sake.

The world tells me that human birth is the worst possible curse. I tell the world that human birth is the best possible opportunity. India's peerless Avatar (direct descendant of God) Sri Krishna has something more to tell the world. He says, "Blessed is the human birth; even the dwellers in heaven desire this birth, for God-Realization is attained only by human beings here on earth."

Dear North Dakotans, dear friends, dear brothers and sisters, I have come to you to speak on the Secret Supreme. I wish to spring a surprise on you. With my soulful joy and in all sincerity, I wish to tell you that your own state and your own university have secretly and most openheartedly taught me the Supreme Secret. The dedicated motto of the state of North Dakota has taught me the Supreme Secret: "Liberty and Union, Now and Forever, One and Inseparable." The aspiring motto of the University of North Dakota has taught me the Supreme Secret: "Light and Law." With your kind permission I wish to say a few words on these two divine mottoes.

To start with the state motto, liberty means responsibility. Whose responsibility? God's responsibility. When a man is liberated from the meshes of ignorance, God acts in him proudly, God acts through him unreservedly, God acts for him unconditionally.

Lord Halifax once aptly remarked, "If none were to have liberty but those who understand what it is, there would not be many free men in the world."

We shall all have liberty, both inner and outer. The inner liberty is the highest realization of the absolute Truth. The outer liberty is the most successful manifestation of Divinity's perfect Perfection on earth.

Union, man's union with God: God is consciously and fully aware of it. Before long he too will be consciously and fully aware of this union. In man's union with God, we see man the soulful gratitude. In God's union with man, we see God the Compassion-Flood.

Now and forever: once liberty has given birth to man's union with God, or man's union with God has given birth to his liberty, man's life starts living forever in the Eternal Now.

One and inseparable: Liberty and union are inseparable because they have to enlighten each other. Now and forever are inseparable because they have to feed each other. Man and God are inseparable because they have to fulfill each other.

It is time for us to dive into the life-growing and soul-fulfilling sea of the university motto: *Lux et Lex* (Light and Law).

Light is not a theoretical knowledge, but a practical wisdom. Law, the Divine Law, is not a command, but an experience. Man's inspiration expands through the bliss of Light. Man's aspiration ascends through the peace of Law. The spiritual Light has an inner glow that illumines the outer life. The unspiritual light has an outer glare that obscures the inner life. When an aspirant lives in Light, he is the doer. When an aspirant lives in the Divine Law, he is the knower. The difference between an ordinary man and an aspirant is this: an ordinary man wants to be defended by the law, although he himself will not care for or follow the law, whereas an aspirant will soulfully, unreservedly and unconditionally defend the law. Law is truth. We have to know how to use the truth in our daily activities.

> A truth that is told with bad intent
> Beats all the lies you can invent.
> —William Blake

This is true, absolutely true. We must always tell the truth with a divine intent. Our truth must be flooded with love, concern and oneness. Our truth must illumine and not blind. Our truth must liberate and not bind. Finally, I wish to say with regard to the university motto that Light is the weight of the universal Soul, and Law is the height of the transcendental Soul.

The Secret Supreme. If you want to realize the Secret Supreme, you have to meditate. You have to know how to meditate. And for that you need a spiritual teacher. Until you have a teacher of your own, you have to meditate all alone. During your meditation, do not be afraid of anything. Fear is something you can and must give up. God's constant Love is something you can and must have. Your fear kills God's Love. Your aspiration for God-Realization and your surrender to God's Will kill all your fear, born and yet to be born. Harbor divine confidence in the inmost recesses of your heart. Confidence is the secret of success. Hope is the secret of attempts. Doubt is poison. Doubt destroys your life of aspiration sooner than immediately. During your meditation, do not fight against evil thoughts. If you constantly fight against evil thoughts, you will, to your great surprise, only strengthen them. But if you open yourself to divine thoughts, evil thoughts will have no need for you. They will be terribly jealous of your divine thoughts and in no time will leave you. During your meditation, try to cultivate divine Love. Try to love humanity soulfully. You may say, "How can I love others when I do not know how to love myself?" I will tell you how you can love yourself. You can love yourself most successfully just by loving God unreservedly. You may ask, "How can I love God when I do not know what Love is?" I will tell you what Love is. Love is the transforming power in our human nature. Love transforms our life of stark bondage into the life of mightiest freedom. Love cries for Life. Love fights for Life. And, finally, Love grows into the Life Eternal.

The Secret Supreme is God-Realization, nothing more and nothing less. Yesterday my ignorance unconsciously offered me to God. Today my knowledge consciously offers God to me. In my unconscious awareness of God, neither God nor I am fulfilled. In my conscious oneness with God, both God and I are fully fulfilled.

TOP SECRETS

The biggest secret
Came out of my little mouth:
    God is still alive.
The sweetest secret
Came out of my little mouth:
    God loves me.
The purest secret
Came out of my little mouth:
    God is for all,
        Including me:
        My uselessness,
        My unwillingness.

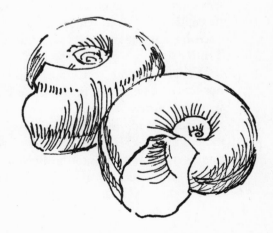

MYSTICISM

University of Minnesota, Minneapolis, Minn.

May 7, 1969

Study mysticism if you want to. It will give your heart joy, your mind inspiration and your life a true, fulfilling and soulful assurance. But do not try to define it. Do not try to interpret it. If you try to define mysticism, you are bound to fail. If you try to interpret mysticism, you will most deplorably fail.

We get experiences: from science, scientific discoveries; from history, historical revelations; from philosophy, philosophical data; from religion, religious doctrines. In these experiences, we see the presence of subject and object, essence and existence, vision and reality. But a mystic experience, which is immediate oneness, transcends all such distinctions. This experience is the constant oneness with the Beyond, the ever-transcending Beyond that always remains ineffable. Mysticism, poor mysticism! When it is oversimplified and underestimated, it comes down from its original sphere and stands beside religion. But even here if a person is sincere, he will realize that his highest religious experience is nothing more than an uncertain, obscure and faint perception of Truth; whereas, no matter what kind of mystical experience he has, he will feel the intensity, immensity and certainty of Truth.

We have also to learn that religious ecstasy and mystical ecstasy do not play the same role in our inner life. Religious ecstasy deals mostly with the human in us. This ecstasy is confined to the body-consciousness, the disciplined or undisciplined vital, the illumined or unillumined mind, the pure or impure heart. But the mystical ecstasy transports us at once into the Beyond, where we are embraced by the eternal Life, fed by the all-nourishing Light and blessed by the transcendental Truth.

Primitive religion offered ecstasy to the vital in the physical mind and in the desiring heart. Mysticism fully advanced is now offering its ecstasy in infinite measure to the liberated souls and in abundant measure to the souls who are on the verge of liberation.

Poor Hinduism. Whenever and wherever mysticism is looked down upon, Hinduism is considered the main culprit. There are many sophisticated Westerners who not only fail to understand the lofty Hindu mysticism, but badly misunderstand it. To them I want to say that Hindu mysticism is not, as they think, self-hypnotism or self-deception, but rather soulful oneness with Immortality's Life, Infinity's Heart and Eternity's Breath. To know Hinduism well, one has to practice Yoga, usually under the direct guidance of a spiritual adept.

Mysticism in Buddhism has been considerably inspired and influenced by Hindu mysticism. Hence, far from being diametrically opposed, the two traditions practically come to realize the same Truth. Nirvana transcends pain and pleasure, birth and death. The blessedness of Nirvana is the highest mystic oneness with the Liberator. A Hindu mystic, on the strength of his self-realization, also becomes one with the Absolute and is freed forever from the snares of pleasure and pain, birth and death.

The Sufi mysticism of Islam expresses itself in the strongest intoxication of the inner vital and in the truth-laden symbolic love between bride and bridegroom. This kind of mysticism perhaps brings one considerably closer to the actual possibility of experiencing oneness with the One. Yet it also wants to tell us that the Allah of the Koran demands a strict self-discipline and a self-controlled life. According to its adherents, this mysticism eventually leads to free access to Him, which is a very rare achievement.

The glowing mysticism of Judaism is the Kabbalah. This mystic lore is founded on the occult interpretation of the Bible and it has been successfully handed down as an esoteric doctrine to the initiated.

Christianity owes its mystical urge, not to Judaism, but to the Greek world. Some scholars are of the opinion that the New Testament is wanting in mystical experience. I find it difficult to agree with them. I wish to say that the New Testament is replete with mystical experiences. What they are actually missing in the New Testament, because of their inability to enter into the depth of its messages, is the key that opens the mystical door that leads to union with God.

In Spain, Teresa of Ávila offered to the world something profoundly mystical. Her mystical experience is the most successful culmination of the divine marriage between the aspiring soul and the liberating Christ, and it is here that man's helpless crying will and God's omnipotent all-fulfilling Will embrace each other.

Mysticism is not the sole monopoly of Hinduism. Christianity and other religions also discovered the Wealth of mysticism.

REVELATION

No more my heart shall sob or grieve.
My days and nights dissolve in God's own Light.
Above the toil of life my soul
Is a bird of Fire winging the Infinite.

I have known the One and His secret Play;
And passed beyond the sea of Ignorance-dream.
In tune with Him, I sport and sing,
I own the golden Eye of the Supreme.

Drunk deep of Immortality,
I am the root and boughs of a teeming vast.
My Form I have known, and realized,
The Supreme and I are one—all we outlast.

THE INNER VOICE

Syracuse University, Syracuse, N.Y.
October 1, 1969

> I would be true, for there are those who trust me;
> I would be pure, for there are those who care;
> I would be strong, for there is much to suffer;
> I would be brave, for there is much to dare.
> —Howard Arnold Walter

To be true, pure, strong and brave, what we need is the Inner Voice. Our Inner Voice is the Truth-Power within us. Our outer voice is the money-power without. Man is not pure enough to see the Truth-Power operating in his outer world of desires and demands. Man is not fortunate enough to see the money-power operating in his inner world of aspirations and needs. The Truth-Power used for humanity and the money-power used for divinity can and will change the face of the world. Truth-Power will awaken and illumine slumbering and unlit humanity. Money-power will serve and fulfill the yet unfulfilled divinity on earth.

The Inner Voice is the heart's wealth. When an aspirant uses this wealth, it soulfully smiles. When an unbeliever and disbeliever in God attempts to use this wealth, it is mercilessly suffocated.

The Inner Voice tells us to help the world only in accordance with God's express Will. If help is rendered otherwise, it is bound to turn into dire calamity later on. He is not only divinely liberal but supremely blessed whose help to another is God-inspired and God-ordained.

To give on second thought a thing requested is to give once. To give a thing for the asking is to give twice. To give a thing unsought is to give thrice. To give a thing when God wants it to be given is to give the thing for good, along with one's own body and soul.

We shall never hear the Song of the Inner Voice if we consciously or unconsciously make friends with anxiety. What is anxiety? Anxiety is the destructive breath of life's poverty.

There can be no greater choice or higher prize than to listen to the Inner Voice. If we willfully refuse to listen to the Inner Voice, our false gains will lead us to an inevitable loss. And if we listen soulfully to the Inner Voice, our true gains will not only protect us from imminent Destruction but will surprisingly hasten our realization of the transcendental Truth.

An aspirant must realize that the Inner Voice is not a gift, but an achievement. The more soulfully he strives for it, the sooner he unmistakably owns it.

Sincerity tells man he should be truly proud that he has the all-discerning Inner Voice. Humility tells man he should be supremely proud that the wrong-shunning, the right-performing and the good-fulfilling Inner Voice has him.

The Inner Voice is at once man's untiring guide and his true friend. If a man goes deep within, the Inner Voice will tell him what to do. If he goes deeper, the Inner Voice will give him the capacity. If he goes still deeper, the Inner Voice will convince him that he is doing the right thing in the right way.

There is a word that is very sweet, pure and familiar to us. This word is *conscience*. Conscience is another name for the Inner Voice. Divinely inspired is the utterance of Shakespeare: "I feel within me a peace above all earthly anxieties, a still and quiet conscience."

Conscience can live in two places: in the heart of truth and in the mouth of falsehood. When conscience strikes us once, we must think that it is showing us its unconditional love. When it strikes us twice, we must feel that it is showing us its unreserved concern. When it strikes us thrice, we must realize that it is offering us its boundless compassion to prevent us from diving deep into the sea of Ignorance.

Rousseau says something quite striking: "Conscience is the voice of the soul, as passion is the voice of the body. No wonder they often contradict each other."

Conscience and passion need not contradict each other if man aspires to offer his heart's light to his passion and his heart's surrender to his conscience. In this way, he can easily transcend this apparently irreconcilable contradiction. Once man has transcended all contradiction, he can powerfully sing with Whitman: "Do I contradict myself? Very well, then I contradict myself. (I am large, I contain multitudes.)"

If you want to be a good man, then contradict yourself when sincerity demands. If you want to be a great man, then don't contradict yourself even when necessity demands.

Fear asks, "Is it safe?" Doubt asks, "Is it true?" Conscience asks, "If not God, who else? What else?"

The Inner Voice is the Temple within us. The Inner Voice is the Deity within us. The Inner Voice is the divine Duty within us. The Inner Voice is the supreme Necessity within us.

God has commanded the Inner Voice to be the friend of aspiring souls and the judge of unaspiring souls.

The Inner Voice is not only constant constancy, but also perfect Perfection.

NOT POWER, BUT ONENESS

State University of New York at Oswego
October 1, 1969

Man has countless desires. When his desires are not fulfilled, he curses himself; he feels that he is a failure, hopeless and helpless. He wants to prove his existence on earth with the fruits of his desires. He thinks that by fulfilling his desires he will be able to prove himself superior to others. Yet, alas! he fails, he has failed and he shall fail. But God comes to him and says, "My child, you have not failed. You are not hopeless. You are not helpless. How can you be hopeless? I am growing in you with My ever-luminous and ever-fulfilling Dream. How can you be helpless? I am inside you as Infinite Power."

Then man tries to discover something else in order to prove his superiority. He tries to exercise his power violently, aggressively. He wants to derive joy from his superiority. He wants to prove to the world that he is important. In order to prove his eminence he adopts any means, and his conscience does not bother him. God, out of His Infinite Bounty, again comes to him and says, "This is a wrong choice. You cannot prove to the world that you are matchless, unique. What you actually crave from your superiority is joy, boundless joy. But this boundless joy will never be yours unless you know the secret of secrets. And that secret is your indivisible oneness with each human being on earth."

Then God continues. He says that He is Strong, He is Happy, He is Fulfilled just because He is totally one with each human being, with the entire universe. Only when one is totally united with the rest of the world can he truly be happy. And this happiness makes a man the unparalleled soul on earth. It is not power that makes us superior or makes us feel that we are priceless; it is our matchless oneness with God. Others do not need us because we have power. No, others badly need our soul's oneness. And this soul's oneness has to be brought into the oneness of the physical, the vital and the mind in an illumined and transformed way. We are great, we are greater, we are greatest only when we consciously feel our oneness with the entire world. And God is eager, He is sincerely eager to prove to the entire world that His aspiring, dedicated, devoted children are truly His Boundless Pride. We do not need to prove what we have and what we are. God is eager to prove to the world what His aspiring children, His dedicated, devoted, surrendered children have and are.

God will fulfill His task in us, through us, for us. Let us also try to fulfill our task. Let us try to have the conscious feeling of our indivisible oneness with each human being here on earth and there in heaven.

What Abraham Lincoln says about power is undeniably correct: "Nearly all men can stand adversity; but if you want to test a man's character, give him power."

And to those who are trying to feel oneness with the entire world, Winston Churchill has something to say: "It is no use saying, 'we are doing our best.' You have got to succeed in doing what is necessary."

Our heart's sincerity never fails. Our soul's concern never fails. Our God's Compassion never fails. When our heart is soulful, our soul is fruitful, our God is meaningful.

I BELIEVE IN ONENESS

I believe in oneness.
A child adds his achievements
To his parents' achievements.
Thus the three become one.
Here I hear the song of oneness,
Here I see the dance of oneness,
Here I feel the reality of oneness.
But for me to say
    A child's achievements
     Equal his father's achievements
        Or
     His mother's achievements
Is sheer stupidity.

You are on top of the life-tree,
He is in the middle of the life-tree,
I am at the foot of the life-tree.
How can our achievements
Be equal?
But we are one,
Undoubtedly one,
Because we have established
Our inseparable oneness
With the life-tree.

I LONG TO BE ONE

    I long to be one
With the Dust of Your Feet.
    I long to be one
With the Smile of Your Eyes.
    I long to be one
With the Love of Your Heart.
    I long to be one
With the Oars of Your Boat.
    I long to be one
With the Glow of Your Promise.
    I long to be one
With the Flow of Your Life.
    I long to be one
With the Victory of Your Banner.

INDIVIDUALITY AND PERSONALITY

University of California, Berkeley, Calif.
October 16, 1969

Human individuality is a self-torturing personality.
Divine individuality is a self-discovering personality.

Man does not have to lose his individuality and personality. Man has to feel and realize his all-pervading divine individuality and all-serving divine personality. When we speak of individuality, we immediately see that it is composed of pride, vanity, desires, frustrations, fear, anxieties, worries and so forth. This kind of individuality can be observed in our ordinary day-to-day life. But there is another kind of individuality, which we call the divine individuality. Divine individuality is totally different from the individuality of pride, vanity, ego, earthbound desires, limited achievements and limited fulfillment. Divine individuality is a direct expression of the Divine in us.

God is One. At the same time, He is Many. He is One in His highest Transcendental Consciousness. He is Many here on earth in

the field of manifestation. At the Highest, He is Unity. Here on earth, He is Multiplicity. God is the Lotus, and He has many, many petals, each representing an individual aspect of Himself. He is manifesting Himself in infinite ways and in infinite forms.

When we speak of human personality, we immediately think of something coming from our physical consciousness or the physical body. A man, with his inborn capacities, tendencies and talents and all his characteristics, forms a kind of personality. When a man stands in front of me, his personality spreads like water flowing onto a flat surface. When we think of a person or a thing, immediately our own individuality enters into the personality of that person or thing. Right now I am here with you at Berkeley, the august university. But if my mind carries me to someone in India, my own individuality immediately becomes one with the person there. I have entered into the person who is now in India, and I can use his personality on the strength of my union with him. I have not lost my individuality. I feel that my individuality has been transformed into an all-pervading and all-serving personality. The moment I think of anybody, my consciousness enters into him and pervades him. When my consciousness takes me into a person I become part and parcel of him. Then I expand my consciousness there. When my consciousness expands, his consciousness also expands. We always serve the moment we consciously enter into something other than ourselves.

In our true Self we are all one. But in our outer self, we are many. Among the "many," we see that one is serving the other; and the "other" may not take an active or even a conscious part in the process. For example, I am giving a talk here. You may feel that I am serving you with my knowledge and my spiritual light, but I wish to tell you that you are also serving the Supreme in me through your communion with me and your understanding and appreciation of my offering to you. This is what we call the all-serving personality. The moment we stand before a person, even if he does not take an active or dynamic part in the interchange, our very presence constitutes an important part of the consciousness of that person. An ordinary person does not understand the language of a flower, but when he stands in front of a flower, what actually happens? He appreciates its beauty, and the beauty of the flower appreciates his consciousness. There is mutual appreciation, mutual love, mutual service.

I am serving you with all that I am and all that I have. You are serving me by becoming totally one with my consciousness. That is true service. In this kind of service we do not lose our individuality. My individuality remains inside you, and your individuality remains inside me. It is the extension of our personality in the form of this widened individuality which the Supreme expresses in infinite ways. Although a tiny drop of water can be taken as an individual drop, when it merges into the infinite ocean it does not lose its so-called individuality. On the contrary, its individuality is expanded into an infinite expanse of ocean. When we look at the ocean we see the ocean as an immense being, a huge personality that has inside it billions and billions of living beings. It is a living being itself. By merging into the ocean, the drop becomes as great as the ocean. Similarly, when we enter with our individuality into our divine personality, we see that our individuality is transformed into the infinitely vast and all-pervading personality of the Divine.

WHO'LL BUY MY GIANT PRIDE?

In vain I try to sell my giant pride;
　　No soul ventures to come forth.
My beloved Lord, You try!
　　This vital horse only You can ride.
The more my bosom aches, the more it grows.
　　My hunger plays the fool,
My ignorance knows no school.
　　The night of destruction piercing flows.

THE SUNLIT PATH

University of California at Santa Cruz
October 17, 1969

In the spiritual life, the name of the sunlit path is Devotion. This path is definitely the shortcut to God-Realization. It is true that God and His Mysteries are beyond the comprehension of speech and intellect. But it is equally true that God is easily accessible through Devotion.

A true devotee gets great joy when he feels, "All this am I."
He gets greater joy when he feels, "All this art Thou."
He gets the greatest joy when he feels, "Thou art the Master; I am only the instrument."

He who follows the Path of Knowledge says to God, "Father, I want You."
He who follows the Path of Devotion says to God, "Father, I need You."
The former says to God, "Father, I own You."
The latter says to God, "Father, You own me."

A real devotee is a true lover of God. Impossibility has no meaning and can never have any meaning in his life.

As in other paths, in the sunlit path the devotee learns that it does not matter *how long* he prays and meditates, but *how* he prays and meditates. If he prays and meditates upon the Divine sincerely and unreservedly, then he prays and meditates ten times at once.

When an aspirant starts his journey along the sunlit path, he says to God, "Father, give me."
At his journey's close he says, "Father, receive me."

We all know that the abode of gratitude is the heart. Strangely enough, gratitude often manages to hide from its abode. But in the sunlit path soulful gratitude is always visible, looming large in the aspirant's heart.

Self-love mars the fertile soil of aspiration and renders it sterile. But devotion toward God kindles the mounting flame of aspiration, creating a new world for the aspirant in God, and a new world for God in the aspirant.

Devotion is blessedness itself. This blessedness is the self-dedicating love turned toward God, seeking to serve Him constantly and unconditionally so that He can be fulfilled both in heaven and on earth.

There are countless people on earth who not only claim to pray, but actually do pray. How is it that they get practically no result from their prayers? The answer is simple and clear. Their prayer is not snow-white. A snow-white prayer is the fount of a self-generating energy, a self-transforming light and a self-fulfilling delight.

Like everyone else, a devoted aspirant has needs. But his needs and God's Love and Compassion are always seen together. A real devotee has come to realize that he loves God not to fulfill his human desires but to fulfill God in God's own Way. For an unaspiring person, life is punishment, pure torture. For an aspiring soul, each moment in life is an opportunity for self-illumination and God-fulfillment. In the sunlit path of devotion, the aspirant knows that just as he is hungry for God's Infinite Compassion, even so is God hungry for his constant feeling of conscious oneness with Him.

When the body is dirty, soap is necessary to clean it. When the mind is impure, tears of repentance are necessary to purify it. When the heart is impure, the need for devotion is paramount. The heart's impurity is the most dangerous disease in the spiritual life. Devotion is the only medicine. Devotion is the only cure.

The Brahman is by nature indivisible, a complete whole. But through *maya*, its self-limiting force, it has broken itself into infinite pieces. The aspirant's all-surrendering devotion can easily make him whole again, divinely complete and supremely One.

I ASK FOR THINGS

I ask You for things, therefore I am insignificant
    and destitute.
If not, I could also be Rudra, the Guru of the
    world.
My heart never wants to be as great as You are.
O Lord, if I equal You, then in me the nectar of
    devotion will reside no more.

DEVOTION

When you love
    With devotion,
You are divinely great.
When you surrender
    With devotion,
You are divinely good.
When you pray
    With devotion,
You are supremely great.
When you meditate
    With devotion,
You are supremely good.
Devotion, devotion, devotion.

SELF-KNOWLEDGE

University of San Carlos, Cebu City, The Philippines
October 30, 1969

Let us try to know ourselves. Let us try to observe what we truly are. Very often we feel that we are insignificant creatures. We have nowhere to go, nothing to achieve and nothing to give. This is what we feel in our day-to-day existence. But what we truly are is totally different from what we feel. We are all God's children. At each moment, God is pouring into us something divine and something truthful. He expects much from us, but nothing beyond our capacity. He knows what we can consciously offer to Him. Right now, we feel that we are weak, unimportant, useless. But in God's eyes, we are divine, we are fruitful, we are Infinite.

We are constantly making mistakes. The root of our mistakes is our body, the physical. We feel that there is nothing beyond the physical and, at the same time, that there is nothing in the physical. It is here that we are making a most deplorable mistake. If we go beyond our body, beyond our physical consciousness, we see Infinite Peace, Infinite Joy, Infinite Bliss and Power all eagerly waiting for us.

Then if we go deep within, deep inside our body, we see and feel the soul. This soul is the messenger of God on earth. If we can be in tune with the constant, spontaneous music of the soul, our lives will be free from suffering, misery, frustration, fear and worry. Our lives will be a constant success, a constant achievement and a constant fulfillment, a fulfillment that can and will be both inner and outer.

So either we have to go deep inside the body, into the inmost recesses of our heart, or we have to go beyond the body, beyond the physical sheath, beyond the physical consciousness. We have to discover our true Self, either today or tomorrow or the day after. Mere preaching will not do; book study will not do. If we at all preach the Truth, the gospel, the spiritual philosophy, then we must preach what we live and practice what we want to be. We have to practice what we want to be, and, if we preach, we must preach only what we live.

God's Vision is man and man's reality is God. Man can deny God. His ignorance can make him feel that there is no God and no need for God. But God's Compassion can never deny the existence of man. God is made of Compassion, Infinite Compassion. Man is made of ignorance. Whenever I say "man," I mean the human mind, the human body. For man is in reality the descendant of God. To realize God is man's birthright. Divinity is his heritage. But man is tired, man is frustrated, man wants to live in darkness. Man is very often satisfied with his limitations. So what can God do? If there is no sincere seeking, no striving, no aspiration, God has to lower Himself into this unlit, ignorant human being.

Man needs God, but he denies it. God needs man, and He is proud to tell the world of His need. Man certainly wants to get everything from God, but he wants to give God no credit for His infinite Grace and Compassion. But God openly shows His pride in human achievement. If we are aspiring, we will in no time see and feel the truth of this. God is constantly proud of our achievement, our aspiration, our existence.

So I wish to tell all of you not to cherish the idea that God has failed His Creation, that God has been a failure. These ideas are completely wrong. God has not failed. It is we who constantly feel that God and God's Creation are two totally different things. We think, "God is in heaven and we are on earth. God does not care for us. Or if He does care for us, He has no strength to correct, rectify or perfect His Creation." This is a wrong conception of the Truth. What do we know about God's Perfection, God's Vision, God's Reality, God's Consciousness? With our human eyes, what do we seek? Perfection, achievement, success. To God's Eyes, these things look totally different. Man's success and God's success are not necessarily the same. God's success is experience, and that experience can take the form of either success or failure. He gives us these two kinds of experience.

When we live in the soul, we feel that our soul has all responsibility for us. When we live in the body, we see that our body is nothing but stupidity. So if we live in the soul, we shall have the spontaneous experience of fulfillment. But if we live in the body, we shall have the spontaneous experience of frustration and misery. Our success and our failure have very little to do with God's Wisdom, God's Experience and God's Operation in the physical world. *He* is our failure, *He* is the doer and *He* is the action. If we can see God's presence in each action, and then see the action itself as God, and later the result—success or failure—as God, and finally the Doer Himself as God, then all our problems are over. We can claim ourselves to be God's Pride. We are truly God's highest Pride and Vision if we know the secret of living here on earth and there in heaven.

I CALL MYSELF

I shall now call myself;
I shall now call.
In the forest of my heart, seeing myself,
I shall love myself and love myself.
I shall be my own quest,
My absolute wealth.
The journey of light supreme will commence
In the heart of freedom.

GOD, TRUTH AND LOVE

Southwestern University, Cebu City, The Philippines
October 31, 1969

Because I love mankind, God loves me. Because I love God, Truth loves me. Because I love Truth, I really and truly love myself.

Why should God love me? I just said that God loves me because I love mankind. There is another reason, too. God loves me because I love His entire Creation. I know and feel that God can never be separated from His Creation. Creator and Creation are one, inseparable. When we appreciate the Creation, the Creator is pleased and satisfied. When we ourselves create something, produce something, build something, people notice our achievement and appreciate it deeply. We are pleased because it is we who have done it. Similarly, the universe is God's Creation. When we love the universe, we simultaneously love God the Creator and God the Creation; and both the Creator and the Creation will be pleased with us.

Because I love God, Truth loves me. Truth has no existence without God. God is the very breath of Truth. Truth and God are one, indivisible. On the one hand, Truth is another name for God. On the other hand, Truth cannot exist without God, whereas God can at each moment transcend Truth—earthly truth and heavenly truth, earthbound truth and heavenward truth. Even His own Transcendental Truth God can transcend at His own sweet Will. Although we can safely say that God and Truth are one, God alone has the power to transcend all truths, even the Truth itself. That is why Truth without God is helpless. But when we love God, Truth loves us because Truth is immediately fed by our aspiring soul. Inside God is the existence of Truth. In our very appreciation of God, Truth is fed and nourished. And Truth rightly feels that its unique message to the world can be spread only when we truly love its Possessor, God.

Because I love Truth, I love myself. A human being is the expression of Truth. He is not the expression of ignorance, falsehood, darkness and death. No, he is the embodiment, realization and expression of truth—the lesser truth, the higher Truth and the Highest Truth. Each moment the divine Truth is transcending its boundaries in us. We see it, feel it and realize it when we live the inner life, the life of the soul. Because I love the Truth, I really and truly love myself. My existence and Truth are the obverse and the reverse of the same coin, which is the inner being or soul, the representative of the Supreme here on earth.

I love myself. What do I love about myself? Not my body. If I love my body for the sake of my body, tomorrow I shall be frustrated because there are millions and billions of human beings on earth who are more beautiful than I am. Naturally I will feel miserable. If I love my physical mind for the sake of my mind, tomorrow I shall see millions and billions of mental giants right in front of me, and my mental capacity will fade into insignificance. If I love my vital dynamism for the sake of my vital dynamism, then I shall see that there are millions and billions of people who are simply inundated with striking dynamism. Similarly, if I love anything else of my own, for its own sake, I am bound to be frustrated. I shall defeat my very

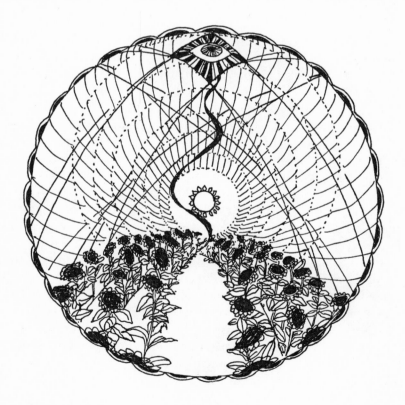

divine purpose. But if I love myself just because God is expressing Himself through this body, vital, mind and heart, then I see that I am unique and peerless in the whole history of the universe, because no other Chinmoy is going to be created by God with the same capacities, same understanding, same experiences. Each individual can love himself just because he is a direct channel of the Divine. God wants to express Himself in each individual in a unique way. When we become consciously and fully one with God, we not only fulfill Him but we also fulfill ourselves. When I say that I really and truly love myself because I love Truth, it means that I consciously feel that Truth is constantly breathing in me, with me and for me.

My very breath on earth is the living reality of Truth. I love and adore myself at every moment—not because of my sound body, dynamic vital, refined mind and pure heart, but because God is inside me, God is utilizing me, God is fulfilling Himself in me and through me. This is the sole reason why my body, vital, mind and heart are loved by me and must be loved by me. Each individual has to be surcharged with this supreme Truth. He should consciously feel that his life on earth is the outer manifestation of the Supreme's inner Breath.

> Supreme, I am Thy Glowing Grace.
> I am Thy Golden Plow.
> I am Thy Vision's Kite.

THEY TALK

Joy talks, but it does not
    Always
Tell the truth.
Love talks, but it does not
    Always
Tell the truth.
Oneness talks, and it
    Always
Tells the truth.
    What is truth?
God's first invention
    And
Man's last discovery.

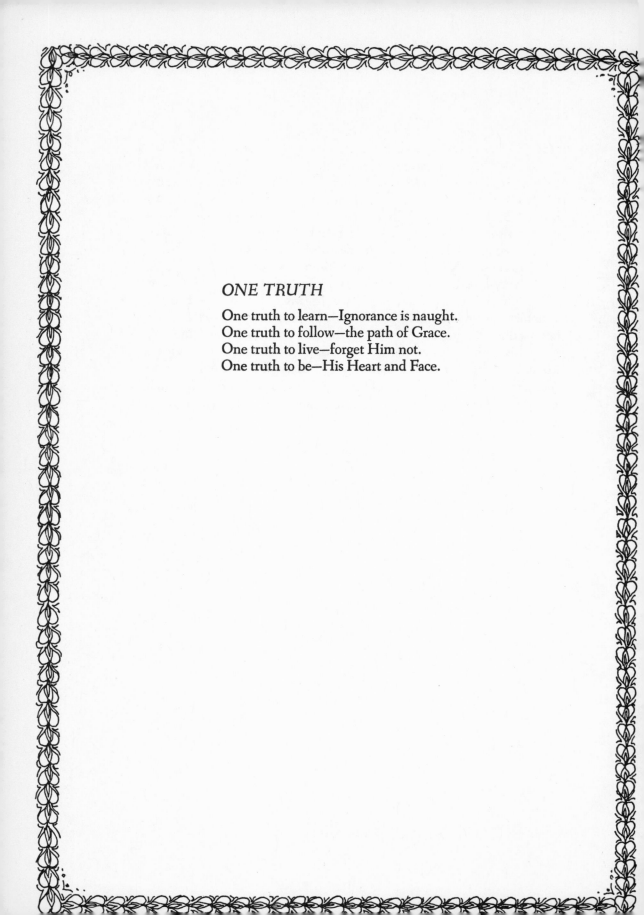

ONE TRUTH

One truth to learn—Ignorance is naught.
One truth to follow—the path of Grace.
One truth to live—forget Him not.
One truth to be—His Heart and Face.

THE BODY'S REALITY
AND THE SOUL'S REALITY

Siliman University, Dumaguete City, The Philippines
November 1, 1969

Today the body is here; tomorrow it is somewhere else. Today the body is suffering; tomorrow the body is enjoying. Today the body is doomed to disappointment; tomorrow the body is surcharged with inspiration and aspiration. The body is constantly seeing and feeling itself in different shapes and forms, feeling that it has no permanent reality.

Despite being real, the body feels that it is unreal. It always tries to discover reality in something else, in someone else or someplace else. The body, being unconscious, feels that it lacks the Truth, the Reality and the Plenitude. It always feels that it is a beggar. According to the body, Reality is something static. And feeling that it is nowhere near the eternal Reality, the body seeks it somewhere else where it is permanent.

Let us take the example of a beautiful girl. Everyone knows that she is extremely beautiful. Beauty is a reality in her. But she is not satisfied with her beauty. She feels that someone else is more beautiful than she, perhaps even someone whom others consider ugly. No matter how many times her dearest ones tell her, "You are the beauty. Nobody is as beautiful as you are," she is not satisfied. This is the case, not only with physical beauty, but wherever reality exists in the physical realm.

The physical is not and cannot be satisfied with its own possessions. It feels that others have the truth, light, beauty and bliss whereas it does not. The very nature of the physical is to feel that it is the eternal beggar. It wants something from somewhere else, either from human beings or from heaven. There is always a sense of dissatisfaction in the physical. The physical is naturally the seat of dissatisfaction.

The case of the soul is not like that, however. The soul constantly feels that it has everything from God in infinitesimal measure and that it has the potentiality to house Infinity. It is satisfied with its reality. The soul is satisfied because it knows what it has and what it can grow into.

The soul now exists in the field of manifestation. It knows that it has the capacity to unveil the Infinite, either today or tomorrow. It is satisfied with what it has right now; and it is also satisfied with what it will have, what it will do and what it will reveal in the Infinite, for the Infinite. The very nature of the soul is to remain satisfied. It lives in divine satisfaction. Very often the body gets joy and still remains unsatisfied. But the soul lives in constant joy, for it sees the Eternal Reality.

The soul is aware of the truth that Reality is both static and dynamic. The soul is satisfied when it sees the Reality in its highest, in its deepest, in its all-pervading consciousness. The body never sees Reality from all angles, never sees Reality in its ultimate sense, the way it must be seen, felt and realized.

The body wants to feel Reality in its own way—that is, by separating it into infinitesimal pieces and seeing it bit by bit. But the soul wants to see Reality in all its phases, in all its activities both dynamic and static, in all earthly incidents and heavenly experiences. The soul does not limit Reality. It sees Reality in its infinity, it feels Reality as the infinite expression of the Absolute and it always tries to identify with Reality in its infinite ways of expression and realization. Although the body is trying to get the highest Reality, which is both static and dynamic, it can never look at or feel the Reality unless it surrenders totally and unreservedly to the wisdom of the soul.

The ordinary human body is imperfection incarnate. This imperfection can be transformed into perfection only when the body voluntarily offers itself to the soul's ever-growing Light, Wisdom and Bliss. A day is bound to dawn when the body will make this offering. Then the body and the soul will run together to fulfill the Supreme's Mission—the mission of nature's transformation, the mission of the revelation, manifestation and fulfillment of the highest Truth here on earth.

ABOVE ALL

Man above all:
This is the height
Of my animal realization.
Love above all:
This is the height
Of my human realization.
Oneness above all:
This is the height
Of my divine realization.
God-manifestation above all:
This is the height
Of my absolute Perfection.

VISION-SKIES

The body
Loves to be swayed by the wind of emotion.
The vital
Loves the prickings of desire.
The mind
Loves the confines of the finite.
The heart
Loves to be in the galaxy of saints.
The soul
Loves the life of unhorizoned vision-skies.

A ZERO AND A HERO

I am a zero.
   Therefore
I pray to God.
I am a hero.
   Therefore
I take care of man.
When I am in the body,
I represent the nothingness
   Of a zero.
When I am in the soul,
I represent the Treasure
   Of Eternity.

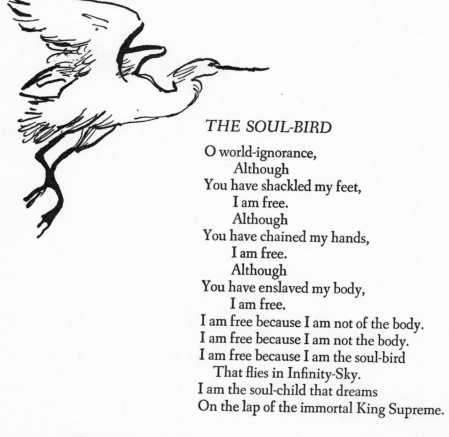

THE SOUL-BIRD

O world-ignorance,
   Although
You have shackled my feet,
   I am free.
   Although
You have chained my hands,
   I am free.
   Although
You have enslaved my body,
   I am free.
I am free because I am not of the body.
I am free because I am not the body.
I am free because I am the soul-bird
   That flies in Infinity-Sky.
I am the soul-child that dreams
On the lap of the immortal King Supreme.

SINCERITY, PURITY AND SURETY

Bucknell University, Lewisburg, Pa.
March 4, 1970

Let us be sincere. The Supreme will bless us.
Let us be pure. The Supreme will love us.
Let us be sure of our Goal. The Supreme will embrace us.

"Let us be sincere. The Supreme will bless us." An aspirant has to be sincere, not only in his inner life but also in his outer life, until he breathes his last. Sincerity is the fertile ground in the aspirant's heart. His sincerity is God's matchless Smile. His sincerity is God's peerless Pride.

Sincerity can be developed. It can be developed like a muscle. There are some people who are naturally sincere, and others who are naturally insincere. Those who are sincere from the dawn of their lives are blessed. But those who are insincere from their very birth need not and must not curse themselves. They *can* be sincere if they want to. The moment they truly want to be sincere, God in His Infinite Compassion will help them. With His deepest Joy, Pride and Concern He will help them.

Spirituality needs and demands sincerity from the beginning to the end. Spirituality and sincerity can never be separated. If one really cares for the spiritual life, if one feels that spirituality is the only answer, then I wish to say that sincerity is the key that opens the door of spirituality. There is no other key; there can be no other key.

"Let us be pure. The Supreme will love us." If there is no purity in the aspirant's inner or outer life, then the aspirant is no better than an animal. Without purity he cannot retain any of the spiritual gifts he receives. Everything will disappear and everything will disappoint the seeker if he is wanting in purity. But if he is flooded with purity, the divine qualities will all eventually enter into him. They will sing in him, dance in him and make him the happiest person on earth. And by making him happy, these divine qualities will find their own true fulfillment.

Purity in the physical is of paramount importance. This does not mean that we have to bathe ten times a day. No, purity is not that. Purity does demand that you have a clean body, but true physical purity lies inside the heart. You have to establish an inner shrine within your heart. This shrine is the constant remembrance of the Supreme Pilot inside you. When you constantly and spontaneously think of the Supreme Pilot seated inside you, in the inmost recesses of your heart, you will realize that this is the *highest* purity. If purity is lacking in the physical, complete success, the full manifestation of God, cannot be accomplished. You may get partial spiritual success, but even this partial success in life will disappoint you badly if purity is not established in your nature. You have to establish purity in the physical, in the vital, in the mind—everywhere in the outer nature. Then whatever you do, whatever you are, whatever you possess will be filled with purity. Purity is not something weak or negative; it is something soulful and dynamic. It is something that is fed constantly by the infinite Energy and the indomitable, adamantine Will of the Supreme.

The very utterance of the word "purity" can help to change the aspirant's outer life as well as his inner life. Repeat the word "purity" one hundred and eight times daily, placing your right hand on your navel as you say it. Then you will see that abundant purity will enter into you and flow through you. When you are pure, you will see the world with a different eye. You will see purity dawning fast in the world. You will see beauty blooming fast in the world. You will see perfection growing fast in the world.

Sweet, sweeter, sweetest is purity. When you see purity inside you, you are pure. When you feel purity inside and around you, you are purer. When you become purity within and without, you are purest. You actually kill your inner being when you lead an impure life. But when you lead a pure life, you expedite the journey of your soul. Your soul and your outer life get their greatest opportunity when purity is totally established in your life.

"Let us be sure of our Goal. The Supreme will embrace us." The difference between an ordinary man and an aspirant is that an ordinary man has no goal whereas an aspirant does. An ordinary man is satisfied with what he has, or considers the idea of entering into the Beyond as beyond his imagination, or feels that there is no Beyond. He is caught by what he sees around him. An aspirant, however, feels and believes that this world of ours is not the final goal. He feels that there must be a goal somewhere, and he knows that either this goal will come to him or he will have to go to it. The goal may be God-Realization or it may be something else. If it is God-Realization and if his aspiration is sincere, he should know that this goal is something absolutely important and sacred. It is not a plaything.

An aspirant has to be sure of his goal. He may want God or some attribute of God. Some aspirants cry to God for Power, for Love, for Peace. They do not cry to God for God Himself. They do not want God in His Infinity and Eternity. They want only a portion of Him. They are satisfied if they can get Peace from God, or Light, or Love. When they receive what they cry for, they end their soul's journey. But there are some aspirants who do not want anything from God except God Himself. They feel that if they get God they get everything. They are like hungry children in a garden where there is a tree laden with the most delicious mangoes. They know that if they can please the owner of the tree they will get all the mangoes on the tree. Here God is the owner of the tree and at the same time He is the tree. When we please Him, He satisfies our hunger for the infinite Light, Peace and Bliss. If the aspirants are wise, they know that the moment they please God they get everything from Him.

On the strength of his sincere aspiration, a true seeker says, "O God, if You feel that I should have Your Vision, if You feel that You want to fulfill Yourself in me and through me, if You feel that You can utilize me as Your instrument, I am at Your service. If You want me to stand before You, I shall come and stand. If You want to stand before me, I shall be equally happy. If You do not want either, but want somebody else to stand before You, I shall still be happy." This is what we call surrender. This is the ultimate surrender.

An aspirant has to know his goal. If his goal is God-Realization, he can start with that in mind. But the Ultimate Goal is unconditional surrender to God's Will. When God sees that His child, His most devoted child, has made this unconditional surrender—not for a second, not for a day or a year, but for a whole lifetime, for all incarnations to come, for all eternity—then alone God embraces His dearest, His sweetest, His most devoted child. And when that embrace takes place, man changes into God Himself.

We are all, without exception, given the opportunity to fulfill God here on earth. If we try, we are bound to succeed. We *can* fulfill God, and in fulfilling Him we shall see that we are already fulfilled.

GOD FEELS

God feels good
When you embody
The life of sincerity.
God feels great
When you embody
The breath of purity.
God feels proud
When you embody
The soul of humility.
God feels victorious
When you embody
The role of His Duty.

WHO CAN STAND?

Against man's impurity,
  Who can stand?
  No, not even a saint.
Against man's insincerity,
  Who can stand?
  No, not even a sage.
Against man's obscurity,
  Who can stand?
  No, not even a seer.
Against man's insecurity,
  Who can stand?
  No, not even a yogi.
Against man's stupidity,
  Who can stand?
  No, not even an Avatar.
Against man's futility,
  Who can stand?
  No, not even God.

SELF-CONTROL

Susquehanna University, Selinsgrove, Pa.
March 4, 1970

In the spiritual life, the most important, significant and fruitful thing is self-control. No self-control, no self-realization. In the dictionary we come across hundreds of thousands of words. Of all these words, self-control is the most difficult one to practice. How can we have self-control? If we want to have self-control, we have to surrender ourselves to the Source. This Source is Light; this Source is God.

A child wants to have many things, many useless, harmful things. But the mother knows that if she gives the child these things he will be ruined. And just because the mother and the child are one, the mother herself will also be ruined. So the mother does not fulfill the child's countless unlit, destructive desires. Similarly, the body is a child. If we fulfill the wants and demands of the body, then in the long run our life will be ruined.

Now, why does the body not listen to us? The answer is very simple. We do not listen to our soul. If we listened to our soul, the body also would listen to us. We know that the body has a superior, which is the vital. The vital's superior is the mind, the mind's superior is the heart and the heart's superior is the soul. The soul's superior is God. The soul listens to the Inner Pilot, God, all the time. The heart very often listens to the dictates of the soul—very often, but not always. The mind practically never listens to the heart. The vital does not listen to the mind, and the body certainly does not listen to the vital. The actual problem starts with the mind, in the mind.

How can we inspire the body, the vital, the mind and the heart to enter into better and more fulfilling light? We have to know at this point that if we find fault with the body, vital, mind and heart, we can never change and transform them. But if we appreciate them, saying that they have the capacity to play a significant role in God's cosmic Drama, that they are as important as the soul for the full manifestation of God on earth, then we can transform them. If we do not condemn the body, vital, mind and heart—on the contrary, if we tell them that they can be the chosen instruments of God, that God needs them for His divine *lila* (game) on earth—then eventually we can transform them. The unruly members of our family will before long feel the importance of their respective roles in the fulfillment of God's manifestation on earth. They can and will be unified and united for the fulfillment of a single Goal.

Self-control. In self-control we need simplicity, sincerity and humility. Simplicity has to feed self-control. Sincerity has to feed self-control. Humility has to feed self-control. We can say that the breakfast of self-control is simplicity, the lunch of self-control is sincerity and the dinner of self-control is humility. Unfortunately, we are living in an age when self-control is not appreciated. It has become an object of ridicule. A man is trying hard for self-mastery. His friends, neighbors, relatives and acquaintances all mock at him. They find no reality in his sincere attempt to master his life. They think that the way they are living their lives is more worthwhile. The man who is trying to control his life is a fool, according to them. But who is the fool—he who wants to conquer himself or he who is constantly a victim of fear, doubt, worry and anxiety? Needless to say, he who wants to conquer himself is not only the wisest man but the greatest divine hero. The Commander in Chief of the cosmic gods, the divine warrior Kumar, son of Lord Shiva, fights against hostile forces, *asuric* forces and ignorance in the battlefield of life. He fights to establish here on earth, in the immediacy of today, the kingdom of heaven. Earlier I said that people mock when a man tries to control himself. At times we see that even spiritual Masters are ridiculed and mercilessly condemned by society. Even a spiritual figure whose heart is snow-white, whose heart is purity itself, whose life has no sting of impurity, whose very breath is the flood of purity—even he falls victim to the criticisms of the ignorant world.

This reminds me of a Zen story. There was a Zen Master who was very pure, very illumined. Near the place where he lived there happened to be a food store. The owner of the food store had a beautiful unmarried daughter. One day she was found with child. Her parents flew into a rage. They wanted to know the father, but she would not give them the name. After repeated scolding and harassment, she gave up and told them it was the Zen Master. The parents believed her. When the child was born they ran to the Zen Master, scolding him with foul tongue, and they left the infant with him. The Zen Master said, "Is that so." This was his only comment.

He accepted the child. He started nourishing and taking care of the child. By this time his reputation had come to an end, and he was an object of mockery. Days ran into weeks, weeks into months and months into years. But there is something called conscience in our human life, and the young girl was tortured by her conscience. One day she finally disclosed to her parents the name of the child's real father, a man who worked in a fish market. The parents again flew into a rage. At the same time, sorrow and humiliation tortured the household. They came running to the spiritual Master, begged his pardon, narrated the whole story and then took the child back. His only comment: "Is that so."

Here I wish to say that in your spiritual life all of you are trying to conquer your lower vital. Either today or tomorrow, in the nearest future or in the most distant future, you are bound to conquer the lower vital. But in the process of your self-transformation, if people do not understand you or care for your pure life, please pay no heed to their criticism. If they do not appreciate your sincerity, your effort or your success in controlling your lower vital nature, no harm. But if you want them to appreciate and admire your attempt, then you are unnecessarily bringing into your life not only their criticism and disbelief, but doubt and temptation as well. Each human being unconsciously embodies criticism, disbelief, doubt and temptation. On the one hand, you are trying to transcend yourself on the strength of your aspiration; on the other hand, you are bringing other people's temptation into your life, and with that temptation you are unconsciously trying to feed your lower nature. So I want you to try to be sincere to yourself. Let the world find fault with you. Let the world bark at you. Your sincerity is your safeguard. Your spiritual discipline will lead you to your destined Goal. Who is the king? Not he who governs a country, but he who has conquered himself. Everybody has the capacity and opportunity to become a king if he wants to. God has given him ample opportunity and boundless capacity to be the king not only of the length and breadth of this world, but of the entire universe.

THE VOYAGER OF SELF-DISCOVERY
THE EMPEROR OF LIFE-MASTERY

I yearn and ache for Thee.
Every day I become
    Love-seed,
    Devotion-plant,
    Surrender-tree.
O Lord, forget me not
    In my outer goal-less wandering
    Far and wide.
O Lord, make my pilgrim-heart
    The voyager of self-discovery,
    The emperor of life-mastery.

SCIENCE AND SPIRITUALITY

Hunter College, New York, N.Y.
March 6, 1970

Man's scientific and spiritual achievements are the conscious inspiration-light and aspiration-might of the Divine's urge toward two goals: the realization of the body's countless necessities and infinite capacities, and the manifestation of the soul's transcendental vision of the Beyond here on earth, in the heart and immediacy of today.

Science is that precious thing on earth which is pushed forward by a glowing imagination and pulled forward by its own growing experience. Spirituality is that precious thing on earth which is carried within by fulfilling aspiration and later brought to the fore, where it can become consciously one with God the Field of Experience, God the Experience and God the Experiencer.

Within our living memory, we have seen science advancing very fast, while human happiness has been receding at an alarming rate. Today's world is seeing a flickering candle-flame of spirituality, but tomorrow's world will be flooded with the light of spirituality, destined and decreed.

Science right now deals mostly with the material world. What is the material world, after all? It is the world that does not believe in the possibility and inevitability of a divine life. Spirituality right now deals mostly with the inner world. What is the inner world? The inner world is the world that says that the possibility of a divine life on earth is undoubtedly unreal today, but tomorrow it will be possible, the day after it will be practicable and just the day after that it will be inevitable.

Science has the capacity to show mankind the full development of the *mental* life. Spirituality has the capacity to show mankind the possibility and inevitability of the life beyond the mind, the *supramental* life.

The outer progress and world-discovery swiftly follow the fruitful imagination in the world of science. The inner progress and self-discovery gladly follow the soulful aspiration in the life of the world within, the world of spirituality.

Science and modern life are simply indispensable to each other. The modern life is the eye; science is the power of vision. Spirituality and the future life of mankind will be indispensable to each other. The future life of mankind will be the fully awakened consciousness, and spirituality will be its guiding and fulfilling soul.

Science itself has become an art, and this art must now stand alongside all other arts. No art can ever have its fullest expression in the modern world without the aid of science. Spirituality is the supreme art of our nature-transformation. God the Supreme Artist uses spirituality to divinely reveal to the world man's embodied divine Reality and transcendental Truth.

To fulfill his practical needs, man bitterly cries to science. To fulfill his personal inner needs, man helplessly cries to spirituality.

The somber despair of ruthless destruction and the matchless ecstasy of the outer, human fulfillment have a common friend: science. The most hopeful certainty of a new and pure creation and the life-energizing, life-nourishing, life-transforming and life-fulfilling delight of the inner and divine fulfillment have a common friend: spirituality.

Science and spirituality must be united. They need each other. Without the one, the other is incomplete, almost meaningless. Together they are not only supremely complete but also divinely meaningful. Science is the Body of God. Spirituality is the Soul of God. Science is also God the Body. Spirituality is also God the Soul. God the Body needs God the Soul to realize Himself, His Individuality. God the Soul needs God the Body to fulfill Himself, His Personality.

> God's Soul and God the Soul say to God in silence, "We loved You before and we shall love You ever."
> God's Body and God the Body voice forth, "God, we love You now and this love of ours will forever last."

> In the world of Night and Fight, Science says to Spirituality, "You fool! You are a perfect nuisance!"
> In the world of Night and Fight, Spirituality says to Science, "You rascal! It is beneath my dignity to speak to a dead stone!"

> In the world of Light and Delight, Science says to Spirituality, "Brother, I need your Wisdom."
> In the world of Light and Delight, Spirituality says to Science, "Sister, I need your capacity."

THE SCIENCE

The science of the Old Man said:
  Look upward, see the Eye of God.
The science of the New Man says:
  Look forward, see the Mind of God.
The science of the God-Man will say:
  Look inward, become
    The Heart of the Absolute.

AGAINST

Against the shore of death,
The waves of science beat in vain.
Against the peak of life,
The arrows of science strike in vain.
Against the vision of the soul,
The soldiers of science fight in vain.

SINCERITY AND SPIRITUALITY

Fairleigh Dickinson University, Teaneck, N.J.
March 11, 1970

Sincerity and spirituality are of paramount importance in our day-to-day life. Human life can be successful only when it is founded on a one-pointed confirmation of Truth in life's multiplicity.

For a God-lover, sincerity is an oasis in the desert of life. It is extremely difficult to be totally sincere, but we need sincerity in the physical, in the vital, in the mental. What is sincerity, after all? Sincerity is the dynamic horse deep inside us, and the rider of this horse is our psychic being.

Thomas Carlyle says, "Try to make yourself honest. If you become honest, then rest assured there will be one rascal less in the world." This is absolutely true. If we can be honest, totally honest, then our lives will have their proper meaning and significance.

Now, what is spirituality? Spirituality is man's inner urge to run toward the Farthest, to fly toward the Highest and to dive into the Innermost.

An unaspiring man will criticize the imperfections and limitations of others although he lacks the inclination, the willingness and the capacity to perfect his own imperfections and limitations. But a man of spirituality is sincere. Not only does he not criticize the imperfections of others, but also he is fully aware of his own shortcomings and he tries to correct them. In addition, he sees the world's imperfections as his very own and tries to perfect them by perfecting his own nature.

Sincerity wants to see the Light. Spirituality shows sincerity what the Light is, where the Light is and how the Light can be seen.

An ordinary person loves the body infinitely more than he loves the soul. A spiritual person loves the soul infinitely more than he loves the body. Why? He knows that his body will last only fifty, sixty, seventy or eighty years, and then he will have to give it up. Each time he reincarnates he is donning a different body, but he has the same soul throughout all his lives. He knows that the soul is the conscious representative of the Supreme, revealing and manifesting in each incarnation the embodied Truth on earth. That is why a spiritual person loves the soul much more than he loves the body.

But an advanced seeker of the infinite Truth will give equal importance to the soul and the body. He knows that he needs the soul in order to enter into the Highest, the Ultimate, the Transcendental Beyond. But he also needs the body in order to manifest the Truth that he achieves in the highest plane of consciousness. He needs the physical in order to manifest the divinity within him. It is here on earth, in and through the body, that he can fulfill God's Vision and God's Reality.

The body we need; the soul we need. The body cries for light, more light, abundant light. The soul cries for God's manifestation, His total manifestation, and for perfect Perfection here on earth.

As the world needs a sincere man, even so God needs a spiritual man. Without a sincere man, the world will be weak. Without a spiritual man, God will remain unfulfilled on earth. Sincerity is God's Heart; spirituality is God's Breath. When we offer our human sincerity to God, God becomes All-Love. When we offer our limited spiritual cry to God, God becomes All-Joy, All-Pride.

With his inner light, a spiritual man can easily succeed here in the material world. This light is his soul-power. This power is not destructive, but constructive. When a spiritual man deals with the outer world, he has no need to fear anybody or anything on earth. His soul-power will always come to the fore to help him establish the kingdom of heaven on earth.

A sincere man is of paramount importance on earth. But his sincerity cannot take him very far. He may be sincere to his friends, to his family and to the world at large; but if he does not have the inner cry, he will not be able to enter into Infinity, Eternity and Immortality. No doubt he is far superior to an ordinary, insincere man. But if he does not feel the conscious need to aspire, if he does not feel the necessity of growing into the Light of the Beyond, if he does not have the inner urge, then for him the Transcendental Goal will always remain a far cry. His aim is only limited perfection, limited joy and limited achievement.

A spiritual person has an inner hunger. This hunger is constant. This hunger is for the Unlimited, for Infinity itself. His dissatisfaction is not the dissatisfaction an ordinary person feels when he does not get what he wants. When a spiritual man is dissatisfied with the world, he is dissatisfied precisely because he feels that the wealth of the world has no real value. He wants Infinity, Eternity and Immortality, and these he will get only from his aspiration. In order to have aspiration, he needs God's infinite Compassion; and he wishes always to bask in the sunshine of God's boundless Grace.

Again, a spiritual person does not look down on a sincere person. He feels that this sincere person is his younger brother. He who has sincerity today has every possibility of entering into the world of spirituality tomorrow.

Sincerity and spirituality should go together. If one has sincerity only, God-Realization will dawn on him in the distant future. But if one has spirituality along with sincerity, then he is destined to realize God very soon. With sincerity's help, slowly and steadily we can go to God. With spirituality's help, we can bring God to us quickly, convincingly and triumphantly.

WILLPOWER AND VICTORY'S CROWN

State University of New York at Stony Brook
March 11, 1970

Lead me from the unreal to the Real.
Lead me from darkness to Light.
Lead me from death to Immortality.
—From the Brihadaranyaka Upanishad

Willpower. What is willpower? Willpower is man's conscious inner urge to enter into the very heart of Infinity, Eternity and Immortality. To live a devoted life is to be a conscious child of God's Will. In the life of aspiration two things are of paramount importance: willpower and prayer.

Prayer is feminine. Willpower is masculine. But both prayer and willpower are most effective, and both can bring about the same result.

Willpower is an ever-progressive and self-manifesting reality in the universe. At times we mortals find it difficult to separate our willing from our wishing. We want to achieve our goal with determined personal efforts, supported and guided by God's loving Grace. Whenever we *will* to achieve something, we pay the price; whereas when we *wish* to achieve something, very often we do not pay the price: we just wish. Here there is no effort, no conscious effort; and so we can hardly expect any success.

Human willpower and divine Willpower. Human willpower is like a rope of sand. At any moment it can break. Divine Willpower is the aspiring humanity within us evolving into the all-fulfilling Beyond.

Victory's crown. Where is the greatest victory? The greatest victory lies in self-discovery. *Atmanam viddhi:* Know thyself. There can be no greater victory than to know oneself. To conquer a nation is a human victory. This victory is limited. When Caesar said, *"Veni, vidi, vici"*—"I came, I saw, I conquered"—he was referring to a human victory. Again, when the Son of God says, "Father, let Thy Will be done," here human aspiration has entered into the infinite Wisdom-Light of the Supreme. The real victory is achieved only when one has established a conscious, inseparable oneness with one's Inner Pilot.

God's Smile is man's victory's crown. And eternal aspiration is the pride of eternal victory. No aspiration, no realization. No realization, no revelation. No revelation, no manifestation of the divine Truth on earth.

You want to live on earth because you have countless desires. You feel there are many things on earth you have to accomplish. But these desires need not be fulfilled, cannot be fulfilled and will not be fulfilled without God.

When you try to discover yourself, when you want to know what you truly are, God's infinite Bounty dawns on you. With your self-discovery, you can reveal God's Omniscience, Omnipotence and Omnipresence here on earth. It is here on earth and nowhere else that God-Realization and God-Manifestation can and will take place.

In order to be surcharged with willpower we need concentration, meditation and contemplation. We have to know how to concentrate. When our concentration is perfect, we then must enter into meditation. When our meditation is perfect, we have to enter into contemplation.

How can we learn how to concentrate? Just by reading books? No, impossible. Books will give us inspiration, nothing more. In order to learn the secret of concentration, one has to go to a spiritual Teacher. You have to come to the university to learn, to cultivate knowledge. Similarly, the inner knowledge also has to be learned from someone. True, the treasure is within you. But somebody has to show you where your treasure is and where your key lies. You come to school to learn, and for each subject you have a different teacher. But in the spiritual life there is only one subject, and that subject is self-realization. And one real Teacher is more than enough to teach you, guide you, illumine you and fulfill you.

Meditation. Meditation also has to be taught, especially in the beginning. At your journey's dawn, meditation has to be taught. Now you are coming to the university. But when you get your degree you don't continue coming. When you yourself have realized God, or when you are far advanced in your meditation, you do not need a Teacher. But only then, not before.

Then comes contemplation, which is the last rung of the spiritual ladder. You can contemplate on the personal God or the impersonal God. It is always easier, safer and more fulfilling to go to the personal God first and to go to the impersonal God through Him.

Willpower and victory's crown. The spiritual life needs only one thing: aspiration. It is our heart's constant aspiration that gives birth to willpower and victory's crown.

Let us all aspire. Ours is the aspiring soul, ours is the fulfilling Goal—here and now, in the immediacy of today.

MY SOUL IS THE PLAYER

My thought is the doubt,
My mind the doubter.
My feeling is the love,
My heart the lover.
My desire is the destruction,
My vital the destroyer.
My ignorance is the sleep,
My body the sleeper.
My will is the play,
My soul the player.

PRECIOUS

Precious beyond measure is God's Will,
    None can undo its Power.
Precious beyond measure are man's tears,
    They alone can hug God's Hour.
Precious beyond measure is man's love,
    Unveiling His Golden Face.
Precious beyond measure is God's Gift:
    His all-fulfilling Grace.

LORD, IF IT IS YOUR WILL

Lord, if it is Your Will,
I shall love my enemies.
Lord, if it is Your Will,
I shall illumine my friends.
Lord, if it is Your Will,
I shall forgive my earthly existence.
Lord, if it is Your Will,
I shall live without You.
          But
If it is Your Will
That I should equal You
And become another God,
          Then
     I shall cry around You,
     I shall sigh within You,
     I shall die before You.
Lord, give me only one boon:
First and last,
     That You will remain my eternal Lord.

THE INNER POVERTY

Fordham University, Bronx, N.Y.
March 18, 1970

You all know what earthly poverty is. But I wish to speak on poverty from the spiritual point of view.

Poverty is a very complicated word. Poverty is not the body's purity. Poverty is not the mind's clarity. Poverty is not the heart's spirituality. Poverty is not the soul's reality. The body's purity is light. The mind's clarity is vastness. The heart's spirituality is height. The soul's reality is delight.

In the physical life, poverty is the absence of conscious effort. In the spiritual life, poverty is the absence of spontaneous surrender to God's Will. Effort in the physical life tells an individual what he can do and ultimately achieve for himself. Surrender in the spiritual life tells the aspirant what God was doing, is doing and will be doing for him.

Poverty is no shame. In the light of perfection, poverty is not a vice—far from it. It is only a limitation. Poverty is not a disease; it is an obstruction. This obstruction can easily be surmounted.

What is poverty, after all? Poverty is misery. What is misery? Emotional misery is the result of the mind's desire. There is also physical misery, which is caused by tensed nerves. When one does not have faith in oneself, that is the beginning of misery. When one loses faith in one's Master, he falls within the damaging breath of misery.

Poverty in our spiritual life does not mean want of money or material wealth. Poverty in our spiritual life means the absence of a conscious cry for God. A man is poverty-stricken in the spiritual life only when he cannot afford to spend a fleeting minute for God. If he cannot spend a fleeting minute for God, then he is truly poverty-stricken in the inner world. An aspirant is really rich when he feels his entire life is for God. He is richer when he sees his breath is of God.

He is the richest man on earth when he discovers that he and God need each other, love each other and are eternally proud of each other. This discovery he can make only when he lives in the soul. His soul constantly brings reality to the fore from the inmost recesses of his heart and places the reality in front of him. His soul makes him feel that he and God are inseparably one. God needs him to manifest His infinite possibilities and capacities on earth, and he needs God to realize the highest Truth of the Beyond.

No man, no aspirant is or ever can be poor if he lives in the soul. The soul is plenitude, the soul is infinity. If the aspirant lives in the soul, he is all aspiration, he is all realization, he is all perfection.

The aspirant's life is inundated with light. Light in his body is his beauty. Light in his vital is his capacity. Light in his mind is his glory. Light in his heart is his victory.

WHY ARE YOU IGNORING ME?

You will make me closer
And pour all Your inner Wealth into me.
Is that the reason, Mother, why You
 have cast me aside, and are ignoring me?
You will shape me with Your own Hand,
That is why right now You are ignoring me so much.

THE SILENT ARE RICH

Satisfied with a little, afraid of the vast,
Narrow are the confines of man's boasting
   and vainglory.
Always preaching, always boasting and bragging,
   turning the ear deaf.
Seven inner seas are now wild and churning,
   each life is tired and sad.
Satisfaction and fulfillment only a dream.
The entire world is filled with suffering and conflict.
The silent, the liberated and the realized are rich
   in their heavenly treasure.
Let man's inner moon of infinite Light get
   total satisfaction
In the sacrifice divine.

I HAVE NOTHING

I have nothing.
I have nothing to show or tell.
I have no spirituality, no worship,
   no meditation, no adoration,
   nothing.
Only around me are inner pangs and
   frustrations,
Dust, clay and ash.
I am satisfied with the world of
   matter and desire.
I am compelled to be satisfied with
   little, very little.
I have nothing.

THE CONSCIOUSNESS OF THE BODY

City College of New York, N.Y.
March 20, 1970

I wish to give a very short talk on the consciousness of the body. To start with, I wish to cite a few words from Sanskrit: *Sannyasa koru karma sadhana.* It means: "We have to practice the inner life, spiritual discipline, here inside the body. Here inside the body we have to live the life of the spirit."

Confusion is the order of the day. Even now we see what can happen. We were supposed to give a talk in a different hall; now we are compelled to be here. Everything seems to have gone wrong. So, when we live in the body, it is often all confusion. When we live in the soul, it is all illumination. The body is right now unlit, undeveloped, and at the same time it remains unprogressive. That is why confusion is running riot.

We must never offer attachment to the physical body. At the same time, we must never offer our contempt to the physical body. If we are attached to the body, then we are immediately caught by the fetters of ignorance, and we will be lost in the mire of bondage. Again, if we offer contempt to the body, the physical consciousness, we will never be fully and totally fulfilled here on earth. It is here, on earth, that we have to realize the Truth, fulfill the Truth and manifest the Truth.

When the hour strikes, that is to say when the soul rings the inner bell within us, the physical consciousness immediately thinks it is time for its enjoyment. The vital thinks it is time to show its capacity in breaking or destroying the creation. Its aggressive or, at best, its dynamic capacity wants to assert itself boldly and show the creation what it can do: how completely, how cleverly, how confidently it can change the plan, the plan that was envisioned in God's Will. The mind thinks that this is the time to doubt God's Creation and at the same time to doubt the Creator, to doubt His very existence on earth. The heart feels, when the bell is rung by the soul, "Now is the time for me to cry, cry for Light, Peace, Bliss and inner Power; the power that fulfills and not destroys, the power of inseparable oneness with God's Creation, with God's entire universe."

When the physical consciousness tries to see the Truth, it usually sees the Truth with tremendous fear. Fearfully and tremulously it sees the Truth. When the vital tries to approach the Truth, it wants to see the Truth by force, by hook or by crook, ruthlessly, without patience. When the mind wants to see the Truth, it sees with the eye of suspicion, doubt, inner turmoil, anxiety and worry. And when the heart wants to see the Truth, it very often sees with joy, delight and soulful prayer.

The body. As an individual, I pride myself on this physical body. What I have and what I am—it is all my body. The body is the only thing I have to show to the world at large. When I feel that my body is the only thing that I am, then I am nowhere near my realization, not to speak of my revelation. If the body is the only thing that I can call my very own, then temptation, sense-pleasure, frustration, destruction also belong to me.

If I can say that the soul is my own, if I become one, inseparably one, with the existence of my soul, then only will I see the purpose of my life, the aim of my life, why I have come here, what necessity God has in me and what work He will do through me here on earth. When I live on earth, I live not because others are living here. Many people live on earth. I live on earth precisely because I have a special aim, a mission on earth. Each individual has to feel that he or she has something special to offer; and this message has to come directly from the soul and enter into the physical consciousness.

As an individual, unlit individual, I boast, I brag. I say, "I have tremendous strength." But look. When an insignificant ant bites me, I am unnerved, I am irritated. When a South Indian mosquito bites me, immediately I become a raving lunatic. A mere mosquito has disturbed my inner poise. I have the strength to destroy hundreds and thousands of mosquitos. But when I am stung by one mosquito, I am totally lost. One mosquito has robbed my body of all its poise and inner strength. I am conquered by a little mosquito or an ant. Why? Precisely because I live in the body.

If I live in the soul, if my consciousness becomes totally one with the soul which is the source of Light and Delight, then mosquitos can bite, ants can bite; the whole world, like a venomous snake, can bite, I will remain unperturbed. I will remain in the sea of silence and tranquillity.

The body, the vital, the mind usually fight with one another. They quarrel, they fight, they never listen to one another. But when the soul asks them to do something, immediately they become one and they unanimously reject the offer, the soul's divine offer. If the soul wants to offer them light, inner light, individually or collectively, the body, the vital and the mind become, at that very moment, inseparable. In collusion they reject the soul's light. In the field of spirituality, they negate their own inner possibilities through their ignorance.

Atmanam rathinam viddhi shariram rathameva tu. In the Katha Upanishad, one of India's loftiest and best-known Upanishads, we come to learn that the soul is the master, and the body is the chariot, and the intellect, or should we say the reasoning capacity, is the charioteer, and the mind is the reins. Now, we need a chariot, we need a charioteer, we need a master of the chariot. Of course, we need a horse, the dynamic energy of the being, but we also need the reins to control that horse, and the reins are represented by the mind. All these we need in order to complete and fulfill our journey.

If we do not enter into the spiritual life, if we do not pay attention to the inner life, then the body is bound to act like a mad elephant, trampling down everything around us. This very body, however, really wants to respect its superiors, say the heart or the soul. This body wants to be the perfect instrument. It is only its conscious oneness with something higher that can make the body feel what it really stands for, how much inner capacity it can exercise in the outer world of manifestation. But either we give undue importance to the body or we give no importance at all to the body. Here we commit a deplorable Himalayan mistake. When we use the body for the sake of enjoyment, sense-pleasure, only to covet, to enjoy, we are misusing the body. We are giving no importance to the soul. At this point we can well think of the great spiritual master named Maharishi Ramana, a great Yogi. "Why do you pay so much attention to the body? Take it as a banana leaf. Eat your meal, which is placed on the banana leaf, and then after you have eaten, just throw away the banana leaf. It has played its part." Again, if we observe the Truth from another angle, we see that if we just throw the body away and pay no attention to it, we do feel that we are not involved in it, but at the same time if we discard the body as a banana leaf, seeing it only as a covering for the soul, then how can the manifestation take place here on earth?

The highest Truth can be realized only here on earth. God-discovery and Self-realization can take place only here on earth. The soul is inside the body. Now it is the light of the soul that has to come to the fore and illumine my obscure, unlit, undivine consciousness. Once my outer consciousness is illumined, then only there is no difference between the inner and the outer. Now there is a yawning gulf between my inner realization and illumination and my outer manifestation. Unless and until the inner realization and the outer life's manifestation go together, we remain incomplete. So let us take the body as the field of manifestation and the soul as the realization. First we have to realize; then we have to manifest. If we have not realized the Truth, what will there be to manifest? And again, if we have realized something and we cannot manifest it, the Truth is incomplete.

Each seeker, each aspirant, already knows that there are two types of consciousness: finite and infinite. Right now the body possesses, or you can say represents, the finite consciousness. And the inner Divinity, or shall we say the soul, represents the infinite consciousness. It is here in the finite that the Infinite has to play its role. What we see without is the song of the finite. And what we become and grow into will be the Song of Infinity.

Now, either the finite has to enter into the Infinite, or the Infinite has to enter into the finite. Which is the easier: the father comes to the baby or the baby comes to the father? Undoubtedly, it is the father who can come to the baby far more easily, because he has the capacity. But when does the father come to the child? Only when the child cries, cries to be near the father.

In conclusion I wish to quote just a line from India's greatest poet, Rabindranath Tagore. He sang, *"Simar majhe nashibo . . ."*

> In the finite, in the bosom of the finite, You are playing Your tune, O Infinity. The melody has enchanted me. Its beauty is unparalleled. Again, it is in me and through me You are manifesting Your Infinity. That is why You are All-Beauty. You are utilizing the finite to express Your Beauty, You are All-Beauty, You are All-Joy, All-Nectar, All-Delight.

THE FINITE MUST INVOKE
THE INFINITE

Alas, if the finite never loves the Infinite,
How can the Infinite destroy the darkness
    from the mind of the finite?
He who does not invoke the Inner Pilot and
    always remains afar,
His life is bound to be lost in the city of
    falsehood and destitution.

CONSCIOUSNESS

The New School for Social Research, New York, N.Y.
April 7, 1970

Consciousness is our real teacher, our dear friend and our sure slave. As a slave, consciousness carries our teeming ignorance to God. As a friend, consciousness tells us what the supreme Knowledge is. As a teacher, consciousness reveals to us the undeniable truth that today's imperfect and unfulfilled man is tomorrow's perfect and fulfilled God.

Consciousness sings. It sings the song of universal Oneness. Consciousness plays. It plays the game of cosmic Manifestation. Consciousness dances. It dances with God's fulfilling Vision within and God's fulfilled Reality without. Consciousness acts. It acts through man's crying, climbing and surrendering aspiration, and God's descending, protecting and illumining Compassion.

When consciousness is all activity, it bows to God the Mother, its Source. When consciousness is all silence, it bows to God the Father, its Source. From the Mother, it gets the mightiest Power to make the supreme sacrifice for the unconscious earth. From the Father, it gets the highest Light to illumine the unlit earth. Consciousness itself is at once Light and Power. As Light, it identifies with the pure inspiration and deep aspiration of our inner world. As Power, it exercises its divine sovereignty over the darkest bondage and the wildest ignorance of our outer world.

The consciousness that the unaspiring body uses is called the hopeful consciousness. The consciousness that the unyielding vital uses is known as the hurtful consciousness. The consciousness that the uncompromising mind uses is called the doubtful consciousness. The consciousness that the uncovering heart uses is called the truthful consciousness. The consciousness that the unlimited soul uses is called the fruitful consciousness.

Aum Anandamayee Chaitanyamayee Satyamayee Parame

"O Mother Absolute of Existence-Consciousness-Delight!" This triple consciousness is the longest length, farthest breadth and deepest depth. The longest length is Infinity. The farthest breadth is Eternity. The deepest depth is Immortality. When consciousness lives in Existence, humanity devotedly receives what Divinity soulfully offers. When consciousness lives inside its own domain, humanity and Divinity lovingly yet surprisingly share each other's experience. When consciousness lives in Delight, humanity is realized and transformed and Divinity is manifested and fulfilled.

Blind is he who does not see the Consciousness-light. Deaf is he who does not obey the Consciousness-right. Poor is he who cannot eat the Consciousness-fruit. Foolish is he who denies the existence of the Consciousness-sea.

I SING, I SMILE

I sing because You sing.
I smile because You smile.
Because You play on the flute
I have become Your flute.
You play in the depths of my heart.
You are mine, I am Yours.
This is my sole identification.
In one Form You are my Mother and Father eternal,
And Consciousness-moon, Consciousness-sun all-pervading.

LIGHT, BLISS AND CONSCIOUSNESS

Light, you have nullified
My yesterday's fear.
    I am grateful.
Bliss, you have nullified
My today's doubt.
    I am grateful.
Consciousness, you have nullified
My tomorrow's pride.
    I am grateful.

THE INNER FREEDOM

Fairfield University, Fairfield, Conn.
April 8, 1970

The outer freedom is to see what we should. The inner freedom is to be what we must. What we should see is the golden face of Truth. What we must be is the flowing Life of God's Vision and the glowing Breath of God's Reality.

The mother of freedom is Light. The father of freedom is Truth. The wife of freedom is Peace. The son of freedom is Courage. The daughter of freedom is Faith.

Freedom rings where Light shines. Freedom rings when Truth sings. Freedom rings if Peace expands. Freedom rings because Courage demands. Freedom rings, hence Faith blossoms.

Somebody said, "When there's more freedom for mankind, the women will have it." This deplorable statement fails to breathe in the inner world. In the inner world, woman and man have equal freedom to cherish the mind's inspiration, the heart's aspiration and the soul's realization. Furthermore, inspiration is woman; aspiration is man; and realization is man and woman both.

We fight for the outer freedom. We cry for the inner freedom. With the outer freedom, we see and rule the four corners of the globe. With the inner freedom, we see the Soul and become the Goal of the entire universe.

True freedom does not lie in speaking ill of the world, or in speaking ill of an individual or individuals. Again, true freedom does not lie in merely appreciating and admiring the world or humanity at large. True freedom lies only in our inseparable oneness with the world's inner cry and its outer smile. The world's inner cry is God the Realization. The world's outer smile is God the Manifestation.

Freedom is expressive. This is what the body tells me. Freedom is explosive. This is what the vital tells me. Freedom is expensive. This is what the mind tells me. Freedom is illumining. This is what the heart tells me. Freedom is fulfilling. This is what the soul tells me.

My outer freedom is my self-imposed and self-aggrandized obligation. My inner freedom is the birthright of my eternal aspiration and my endless realization.

Now, the paramount question is whether or not my inner freedom and my outer freedom can run abreast. Certainly they can. Certainly they must. My inner freedom knows what it has and what it is: realization. My outer freedom must know what it wants and what it needs: transformation.

When the freedom of my life without is soulfully and unreservedly transformed, it immediately becomes the mightiest might and the highest pride of the freedom of my life within.

My outer freedom is my life-boat. My inner freedom is my life-sea. My God is my Pilot Supreme. Today I am my journey's searching and crying soul. Tomorrow I shall be my journey's illumining and fulfilling goal.

My soul of freedom is my God's compassionate and constant necessity. My goal of freedom is my God's smiling and dancing transcendental assurance everlastingly fulfilled.

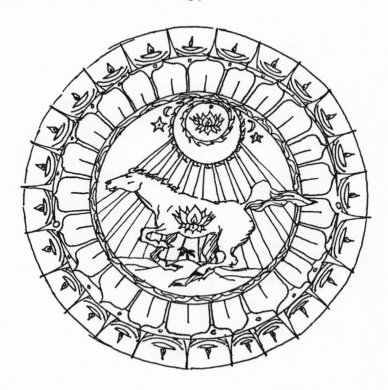

GO AWAY

Go away, go away, go away.
You do not want Divine Delight.
You only want the beauty of bondage.
You do not want the incense-flame of liberation.
O dark enemy, away you go.
For me the dawn of Infinity.

YOU WANT TO BE FREE

You want to be free
From the drag of the flesh.
   You want to be free
From the pull of desire.
   You want to be free
From the push of frustration.
   You want to be free
From the confines of your finite self.
   You want to be free
From the prison-house of your own creation.
Then submit your fear to God's tears.
This is the only way
To regain and safeguard your proudest pride.

EARTHBOUND TIME AND TIMELESS TIME

Long Island University, Brooklyn, N.Y.
April 10, 1970

Time: earthbound time and timeless time. When I look upward, I earn time. When I look forward, I utilize time. When I look inward, I save time. When I look backward, I waste time.

How do I use my time? I use my time serving sincere seekers. When do I use my time? I use my time when God commands my service and man, the aspirant, needs my light. There are only two things: time and life. Time is for life and life is of time. In life, we see God. In time, through time, we become consciously one with God.

Einstein, the world-renowned scientist, said something most striking: "When we sit with a nice girl for two hours, we think it is only for a minute. When we sit on a hot stove for a minute, we think it is for two hours. And that is relativity."

In the spiritual world we come across a similar experience. When we go to a real spiritual Master and drink deep of his divine Peace, Light and Bliss for two hours, we feel we have been with him for only a fleeting minute. And when we sit on the stove of wild ignorance for just a fleeting second, we feel it is for an endless hour. This is spirituality, an eager aspirant's reality.

Bacon also said something striking: "To choose time is to save time." This is a most significant statement. Now, why do we choose time and how can we choose time? We can choose time by loving time. How can we love time? We can love time by meditating constantly on our life's promise to God. What is our life's promise to God? The promise is that God's Light Divine will grow and glow in human life.

What happens when we save time? Opportunity knocks at the door of Possibility, and Possibility knocks at the door of Inevitability. Possibility says to Opportunity while opening the door, "My child, you are wise." Inevitability says to Possibility while opening the door, "My child, you are no longer your searching soul. Today you have become your fulfilling Goal."

"I am the mighty world-devouring Time." This message is from the *Bhagavad-Gita*, the Song Celestial sung by Lord Krishna. Now, we have to know what is actually devoured and destroyed—ignorance, limitation, bondage, imperfection and death. Sri Krishna has already told the human aspirant, Arjuna, why He has appeared on earth: "Whenever righteousness declines and unrighteousness prevails, I embody Myself, O Arjuna. To protect the good, to destroy the wicked and to establish *dharma* [the code of life], I come into being from age to age."

In our day-to-day human experience we very often feel that time destroys us. Herbert Spencer, on behalf of suffering humanity, says, "Time is that which man always tries to kill, but which ends in killing him." We try to kill time. But what actually happens is that time ultimately kills us, devours us. Our hopes are dashed, our desires are frustrated. When founded on insincerity, doubt, worries and anxieties, our aspiration unfortunately fails to bear fruit.

Earthbound time and timeless time. In our day-to-day life we use earthbound time. This time measures all our activities and can itself be measured—one hour, two hours, three hours. Again, one hour is divided into sixty minutes, one minute into sixty seconds. We can break earthbound time into pieces. We can pick the time; we can be on time. Early in the morning, at six o'clock, we will get up. At eight o'clock we shall be in the office. At eleven o'clock at night we will go to bed. Time is registering our life-activities.

But timeless time is totally different. It is like a river flowing into the sea, merging into the sea and finally becoming one with the sea. On the strength of its oneness, it becomes the boundless vast. Here the finite enters into the Infinite and loses itself. What happens when the Infinite plays its role in the finite?

"O Infinite, in the heart of the finite You are playing Your own melodies. In me is Your Revelation and Manifestation. Therefore ecstasy within, ecstasy without." India's greatest poet, Tagore, sang this.

Earthbound time. The body uses this time. The physical consciousness uses this time. The physical mind uses this time. We can use or misuse this time. But once we use or misuse it, this time is exhausted. We cannot get it back.

The soul uses boundless time. Infinity looms large in this time. And if we are consciously one with the soul, we can use the boundless time, the eternal time. We also can misuse it if we want to. But fortunately our soul will not permit us to misuse this time. And even if we do misuse it, the time still remains boundless, eternal.

In our earthbound time we observe one thing: today we have a headache, tomorrow time cures it. Today we suffer from some ailments, tomorrow we are cured. Time comes to our rescue. Similarly, our soul sees a disease in the earth-atmosphere. The soul itself has no disease, for it is beyond disease, beyond death. But in the earth-atmosphere the soul sees the most fatal disease of all, ignorance: ignorance within, ignorance without. The soul wants to put an end to this ignorance. That is, the soul feels that each human being can swim across the sea of ignorance and finally dive into the sea of the soul's infinite plenitude. The hour has to strike. When it does, it is up to us how we utilize this hour.

The Lord Buddha, teaching his disciples, was reading something from a sacred book. After a while he said, "The evening has set in," and closed the book. Immediately his disciples realized that it was time for them to meditate, so they entered into meditation. On that particular day two newcomers, a thief and a woman of ill repute, had attended Lord Buddha's discourse. The thief immediately decided that it was time for him to go and commit a theft. So he left the place. The woman of ill fame realized that it was time for her to go home and wait for her friends. And this she did. At the same hour a seeker of the infinite Truth enters into meditation, a thief does what he thinks best for him and a woman of ill repute does what she feels best for her.

In our spiritual life also, when the hour strikes, three different types of seekers play three different roles. There are lamentable seekers, able seekers and admirable seekers. Lamentable seekers are those who come to a spiritual Master out of curiosity, because they see that thousands of other seekers are flocking toward him. They have countless problems, and they feel that the moment they come to a spiritual Master all their problems will be solved: family problems, financial problems and other kinds of problems.

The able seekers have faith in themselves and faith in God, fifty percent each. They feel that God is pleased with them, and showers His choice blessings on them just because they meditate. They feel that their realization is due in part to their personal effort and in part to God's Grace, and they are happy when they finally reach their Goal.

The admirable seekers feel that their realization has taken place precisely because God has showered infinite Grace on them. They feel it is God's Grace that has enabled them to realize the highest Truth. Their prayer is, "O God, fulfill Yourself in and through us. If You want us to remain unrealized, unknown and imperfect, we are fully prepared. If You want us to realize the highest Truth, to enter into Infinity, Eternity and Immortality, then we are also prepared to do this. Our only prayer is to please You, to fulfill You, the way You want to be pleased and fulfilled. We reject all personal choice. It is Your Choice that we want in our life. We have one aim, one goal: to fulfill You in Your own way, at Your own Golden Hour."

THE BOAT OF TIME SAILS ON

The sky calls me,
The wind calls me,
The moon and the stars call me.
The green and the dense groves call me,
The dance of the fountain calls me,
Smiles call me, tears call me.
A faint melody calls me.
The morn, noon and eve call me.
Everyone is searching for a playmate,
Everyone is calling me, "Come, come!"
One voice, one sound, all around.
Alas, the Boat of Time sails on.

I JOURNEYED

I journeyed into Time,
I journeyed into Space,
I journeyed into skies,
I failed to see His Face.

I NEED YOU NOT

O Time and Space,
I need you not.
My breath has caught
My Supreme's Face.
O Depth and Height,
I need you not.
My soul has bought
Reality's Light.
O Golden Goal,
I need you not.
My Lord has sought
My Journey's Soul.

THE SONG OF EGO

Adelphi University, Garden City, N.Y.
April 15, 1970

My ego needs.
My soul has.
My ego tries.
My soul does.
My ego knows the problem that is.
My soul becomes the answer that is.
I am not alone.
Within my unlit self:
My ego, my naked death.
I am not alone.
Within my snow-white heart:
My soul, and my Spirit's Flame.

Ego is the thief of thieves. Not to speak of ordinary experiences, even realizations are afraid of this intruder.

To feel the absence of ego is as difficult as to see God's constant presence in oneself.

Ego helps bondage grow. Bondage, in return, helps ego flourish or run amuck.

Self-pity, self-indulgence and egoistic emotional cries are but one shortcoming with different names.

O small ego, O big ego, don't worry. Both of you have God's Compassion at your disposal. As there is no difference between a rill and a river when they run into the sea, neither is there a difference between an ordinary man and an important man when they dive into the Sea of God's Compassion.

Ego is diversity in unfulfilling action. Surrender is unity in fulfilled action, fulfilled manifestation and fulfilled perfection.

Self-advertisement cannot even touch the feet of God-Realization. God-Realization cannot lower itself even to touch the head of self-advertisement.

To think oneself always great is to believe that toil and skill are unnecessary.

No doubt, man is infinitely superior to a wild beast. But he always drinks two bottles of poison: one bottle is ego and the other is doubt. Until he has done away with these two bottles, man is no more than a higher animal.

To strive to do something unique is undoubtedly good, but it is better to know whether that unique thing is what God wants you to do.

The difference between God and man is this: man is the determining I. God is the determined We.

Happy is he who has overcome all selfishness. Blessed is he who sees God emerging from the sea of his ego.

The moment we remove the mirror of self-flattery from our eyes and hold up before us the mirror of Truth, we see a half-animal jumping within and without us.

With your unlit and wild ego do not destroy yourself. Suicide is the worst possible barrier to the goal of self-realization. If you destroy yourself, instead of starting your next life where you have left off in this one, you will have to go back to a much earlier point.

There is one defeat that brings us a greater triumph than even victory does. What is that defeat? The defeat of our ego by our soul.

EGO-PUBLICITY AND FRUSTRATION-FUTILITY

Each of his spiritual children
Was convinced that he saw
    No one but him,
    No one but her;
Loved no one but him,
    No one but her;
Blessed no one but her,
    No one but him;
Admired no one but her,
    No one but him.
He lost his existence
Between their blind ego-publicity
And his giant frustration-futility.

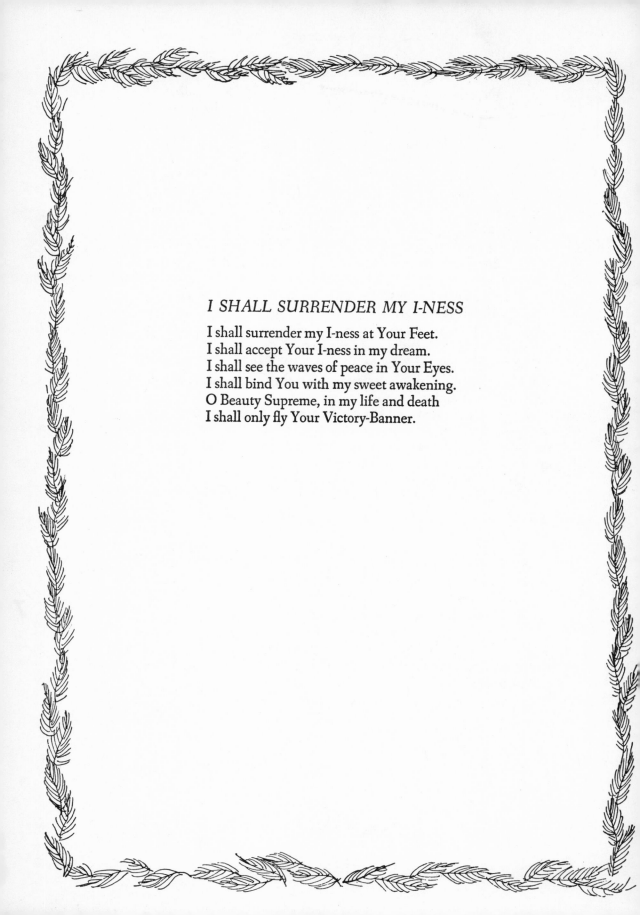

I SHALL SURRENDER MY I-NESS

I shall surrender my I-ness at Your Feet.
I shall accept Your I-ness in my dream.
I shall see the waves of peace in Your Eyes.
I shall bind You with my sweet awakening.
O Beauty Supreme, in my life and death
I shall only fly Your Victory-Banner.

IMMORTALITY

University of Massachusetts, Amherst, Mass.
April 24, 1970

He who does not aspire thinks that immortality is an impossibility. He who aspires feels that immortality is a sure possibility. He who has realized God knows that immortality is an absolute reality.

" 'Impossible!' That is not good French," says Napoleon.

" 'Impossible!' That is not good self-discovery." This is what I say. Today's self-discovery is tomorrow's immortality.

It is good to be immortal, but it is infinitely better to be divine. Socrates said something quite memorable: "All men's souls are immortal, but the souls of the righteous are both immortal and divine."

If divinity looms large inside immortality, then only can reality be all-embracing, all-sustaining and all-fulfilling.

The outer life is humanity. The inner life is immortality. The life around is reality. The life above is divinity. The life below is obscurity.

When divinity descends into humanity, the soul of humanity becomes hopeful. When divinity descends into immortality, the soul of immortality becomes meaningful. When divinity enters into reality, the soul of reality becomes fruitful. When divinity enters into obscurity, the soul of obscurity becomes prayerful.

God inspires man with His immortal Inspiration. Man realizes God with his immortal self-consecration. God meditates on man for his immortal perfection. Man meditates on God for His immortal Manifestation.

To copy others is an act of stupidity. To copy oneself is an act of absurdity. To imitate God is to imitate Immortality. When we imitate God, our life of imagination ends and our life of realization dawns.

How can we imitate God when we do not know who God is? God is the Man Divine, supremely inspiring there in heaven and supremely sacrificing here on earth.

What is immortality? Immortality is the consciousness divine that eternally grows and endlessly flows. While growing, it reaches God the Transcendental; while flowing, it reaches God the Universal.

The body says, "Life is but pressure." The vital says, "Life is but pleasure." The mind says, "Life is the homeland of ideas." The heart says, "Life is the homeland of ideals." The soul says, "Life is the homeland of experiences." God says, "Life is the homeland of immortality."

Mother Earth symbolizes human aspiration. Hence it is a woman in the Upanishads, Maitreyi, who teaches humanity the highest aspiration toward God: "Of what use to me are things that do not make me immortal?"

Let us be inseparably one with Maitreyi and feel that mortality's binding consciousness is bound to be flooded with the boundless consciousness of immortality.

O aspiring man, go deep within. Listen to God whisper, "My child, you are good. Therefore I have made you My Infinity's Heart. My child, you are nice. Therefore I have made you My Eternity's Breath. My child, you are great. Therefore I have made you My Immortality's Life."

MY IMMORTALITY

My beauty
Is immortal in heaven.
My duty
Is immortal on earth.
My aspiration
Is immortal in life.
My surrender
Is immortal in God.

IMMORTALITY

I feel in all my limbs His boundless Grace;
Within my heart the Truth of life shines white.
The secret heights of God my soul now climbs;
No dole, no somber pang, no death in my sight.

No mortal days and nights can shake my calm;
A Light above sustains my secret soul.
All doubts with grief are banished from my deeps,
My eyes of light perceive my cherished Goal.

Though in the world, I am above its woe;
I dwell in an ocean of supreme release.
My mind, a core of the One's unmeasured thoughts,
The star-vast welkin hugs my Spirit's peace.

My eternal days are found in speeding time,
I play upon His Flute of rhapsody.
Impossible deeds no more impossible seem,
In birth-chains now shines Immortality.

INTUITION

University of Maine, Orono, Me.
April 24, 1970

Intuition is a push and a pull. It is an inner push and an outer pull. The push comes from our aspiration. The pull comes from God's Illumination.

When God invites an aspirant to dine with Him, it is the aspirant's intuition that immediately accepts the invitation. The mind is fond of investigation and invention. The heart is fond of aspiration and unification. Intuition is fond of illumination and supramentalization. Intuition tells us in a flash what God looks like. Realization in a twinkling tells us who God is. Intuition, like an arrow, flies toward the Goal. Realization, like an expert dancer, eternally dances in the heart of the Goal.

Intuition is the creation above the mind. Intuition is the freedom beyond the mind. Intuition is the evolution of consciousness-light outside the boundaries of the physical mind.

Again, there is an infinitely inferior form of intuition in the body, the vital, the mind and the heart. The intuition in the body is practically blind. In the vital, it is powerfully obscure; in the mind, surprisingly uncertain; in the heart, deplorably helpless.

The difference between intuition and willpower is this: Intuition sees the truth; willpower wants to become the truth. Intuition has the ability to shorten the road that leads to the highest illumination. Willpower has the ability to bathe in the sea of illumination.

Imagination is not intuition. Inspiration is not intuition. Aspiration is not intuition. But when intuition presents imagination with the truth, imagination successfully expands the truth. When intuition presents inspiration with the truth, inspiration soulfully embraces the truth. When intuition presents aspiration with the truth, aspiration devotedly devours the truth.

Intuition is the golden link between Vision and Reality. Vision needs intuition to carry its all-transforming message to humanity. Reality needs intuition to carry its all-surrendering message to divinity.

ASPIRATION: THE INNER FLAME

Purdue University, Lafayette, Ind.
April 27, 1970

God had a glowing Dream. The name of that Dream was Aspiration. Man has a climbing cry. The name of this cry is also aspiration. God was originally One. With His Aspiration, God wanted to become Many. He wanted to divinely enjoy and supremely fulfill Himself in and through an infinite number of forms.

Man is many. With his aspiration, man the dividing and divided consciousness, man the obscure mind, man the unfulfilled being wants to become one with the world-consciousness, the world-life and the world-soul. He unmistakably and soulfully feels that this is the secret and sacred way to feel the deepest Depth of Reality and the highest Height of Truth.

Aspiration, the inner flame. Unlike other flames, this flame does not burn anything. It purifies, illumines and transforms our life. When purification takes place in our lower nature, we hope to see the Face of God. When illumination dawns in our outer nature, we feel that God is near and dear, that He is all-pervading and all-loving. When our nature, both lower and outer, grows into the Transformation-Flame, we shall realize the truth that God Himself is the inmost Pilot, brightest Journey and highest Goal.

Some people are under the impression that desire and aspiration are the same thing. Unfortunately or, rather, fortunately that is not true. They are two totally different things. The difference between desire and aspiration is very simple and clear. Desire wants to bind and devour the world. Aspiration wishes to free and feed the world. Desire is the outgoing energy. Aspiration is the inflowing light. Desire says to man, "Possess everything. You will be happy." Poor man, when he wants to possess just one single thing, he sees that he has already been mercilessly caught and possessed by everything in God's Creation.

Aspiration says to man, "Realize only one thing, and that thing is God. You will be happy." Fortunate and blessed man, on his way upward and inward, long before he sees God, he feels sublime peace in his inner life and radiating joy in his outer life. He feels that the realization of the Supreme Beyond can no longer remain a far cry.

Aspiration has, not one, but three genuine friends: yesterday, today and tomorrow. Yesterday offered its Inspiration-Flight to aspiration. Today offers its Dedication-Might to aspiration. Tomorrow will offer its Realization-Delight to aspiration.

Aspiration is our inner urge to transcend both the experience and the realization already achieved. This is absolutely necessary because God the Infinite constantly transcends His own Infinity, God the Eternal constantly transcends His own Eternity and God the Immortal constantly transcends His own Immortality.

The childhood of aspiration wants to realize the Supreme in an earthly and individual way. The adolescence of aspiration wants to realize the Supreme in a divine and glorious way. The adulthood of aspiration wants to realize the Supreme in the Supreme's own way.

Aspiration is realization. Aspiration is revelation. Aspiration is manifestation. Aspiration is realization if and when the aspirant needs God-Realization and God-Realization alone. Aspiration is revelation if and when the aspirant feels that God-Revelation is absolutely for God's sake. Aspiration is manifestation if and when the aspirant feels that God-Manifestation is his birthright.

ARISE! AWAKE!

Arise, awake, O friend of my dream.
Arise, awake, O breath of my life.
Arise, awake, O light of my eyes.
O seer-poet in me,
Do manifest yourself in me and through me.

Arise, awake. O vast heart within me.
Arise, awake, O consciousness of mine,
Which is always transcending the universe
And its own life of the Beyond.

Arise, awake, O form of my meditation transcendental.
Arise, awake, O bound divinity in humanity.
Arise, awake, O my heart's Liberator, Shiva,
And free mankind from its ignorance-sleep.

YOUR COMPASSION-WATERS

Peace, Peace,
Peace within my heart reigns supreme.
The Soul-stirring flute of Lord Krishna is
    being played
In my heaven and on my earth.
The destruction-shadows of dark demons
And the ignorance-delusion of somber night
Lie long-buried in the depths of my body,
    mind, heart and life.
My aspiration-flames ever swim across
The expanse of Your Compassion-Waters.

STRIVE

Strive blindly,
And achieve nothing.
Strive carefully,
And achieve something.
Strive soulfully,
And achieve everything.
Strive unconditionally,
And, lo, you have won
    Everything,
Including God.

REALITY

Case Western Reserve University, Cleveland, Ohio
April 28, 1970

There are three realities: God, Soul and Life. God is the Transcendental Reality. Soul is the Inmost Reality. Life is the Universal Reality. God reveals the soul; the soul reveals life. God the Reality lives in His creative Will. Soul the Reality lives in its sustaining Will. Life the Reality lives in its fulfilling Will.

Again, God's Realization embodies His creative Will. His Concern shelters the soul's sustaining Will. His Compassion feeds the life's fulfilling Will.

Reality is the constant and dynamic process of our inner evolution. The Reality of the past is growing. The Reality of the present is soaring. The Reality of the future will be glowing.

Real Reality is not an escape from life. It is the acceptance of life, the expression of life and the interpretation of life. When we accept life, we become divine warriors. When we express life, we become conscious representatives of God. When we interpret life, we become God's eternal pride.

Reality is at once the expansion of our human consciousness and the essence of our divine consciousness. Human consciousness shakes hands with possibility and ability. Divine consciousness embraces faith and surrender. The flowering of human consciousness is Realization. The flowering of divine consciousness is Manifestation. The human consciousness thought that God was unknowable. Now it feels that God is merely unknown. Soon it will realize that God is unmistakably and unreservedly knowable. The divine consciousness knows that there was nothing, there is nothing and there can be nothing other than God.

Faith is the simple, direct, effective and complete form of Reality. Doubt is the complex, indirect, ineffective and incomplete form of

Reality. Faith is God-comprehension. Faith is God-description. Doubt is Truth-detention. Doubt is Life-suffocation.

> Reality's unity is God's existence.
> Reality's multiplicity is God's experience.
> Reality's singularity is God the Eternal Lover.
> Reality's plurality is God the Eternal Love.
> Reality's Time-age is Eternity.
> Reality's Experience-age is Infinity.
> Reality's Realization-age is Immortality.

A SWEET LONGING

A sweet longing have I
For the mainland of Reality.
No more shall I live
A life founded upon
Culled fictions.
Splintered, broken and smashed
Realities of life
No more can torture my intrepid heart.
From now on in my mind
Only God-Reality will grow.
In my heart
Only God-Love will grow.
In my life
Only God-Embrace will grow.

REALITY'S IMMORTALITY

Thousands of years ago
He cried for the Throne.
Hundreds of years ago
He saw the Throne.
Two hundred years ago
He touched the Throne.
One hundred years ago
He sat on the Throne.
He was captured by Divinity's Beauty.
Now he has become the Throne.
He is claimed by
Reality's Immortality.

A YAWNING GULF

A yawning gulf between
My vision-tree and my reality-plant.
A yawning gulf between
The place I love to live and the place I live.
I love to live under the vault of heaven.
Alas, my existence lives
In the valley of the shadow of death.
Peace has escaped my remembrance;
Delight, too.
But I know a swing of the pendulum
Will change my face and fate.
My surrender supreme
Shall marry my dream-boat
With my reality-shore.

I LIVED

I lived in the cottage
    Of Dreams
To see the Face of Reality.
I live in the house
    Of Dreams
To shake hands with Reality.
I shall live in the Palace
    Of Dreams
To become the Soul of Reality.

LOVE AND BECOME

I looked for the mainland
    Of Reality,
And I found it.
    It whispered:
    "Love or suffer,
    Love or die,
    Love and grow,
    Love and become.
The world of hesitation has frightened your heart.
The world of calculation has puzzled your mind.
The world of temptation has captured your vital.
The world of depression has devoured your body."

SELF-CONTROL: SELF-OFFERING TO GOD

York University, Toronto, Canada
October 7, 1970

Self-control does not mean self-torture. Neither does it mean austerity. Unfortunately, in the West, self-control has been misunderstood. People think that the austere, arduous life practiced by some Indian aspirants of the past stands as the ideal of self-control. But that kind of austere life, torturing and punishing the body, is not real self-control. It is self-mortification. It leads us to abysmal destruction in the heart of ignorance. If somebody wants to realize God by fasting for days and months, then he will be embraced by death, not by God. A normal, natural life—the middle path—is what God demands from us. The Buddha taught us to follow the middle path, not to go to extremes. We have to be very firmly planted on earth. The root of the tree is under the ground, not elsewhere. The root is under the ground, and the branches are looking up toward the highest. So self-control is within and self-manifestation is without. Self-control leads us to self-illumination. Today's self-control will be tomorrow's self-transcendence.

For self-mastery, self-control is of paramount importance. Self-control takes time. It cannot be achieved overnight. Through self-introspection, self-examination and proper meditation, one achieves self-control.

I wish to tell about an incident in the life of Socrates. Once Socrates and a host of his admirers went to see a palmist. The palmist read Socrates' hand and said, "What a bad person you are, ugly and full of lower vital problems. Your life is full of corruption." Socrates' admirers were thunderstruck. They wanted to strike the palmist. What gall he had to say such things about Socrates, who was truly a pious man, a saint. But Socrates said, "Wait, let us ask him if he has said everything." Then the palmist continued, "No, I have something more to say. This man has all these undivine qualities, without doubt, but they are all under his control. He has not shown any of them. They are all under control."

Before one gets illumination, he may be attacked by all the undivine forces of the lower vital. But he can easily place them at his feet. Socrates did it. Any aspirant can easily conquer these wrong forces after a while. Countless times he may be attacked by vital impulses. Each time he can play the man. He can manfully, boldly, courageously place his feet on the heads of these dark forces. The golden day will come when illumination dawns on life, and then everything will be transformed. Emotional problems will be transformed, becoming the dynamic strength of the divine for the divine to use. But until then the aspirant has to fight hard.

Ramakrishna used the phrase "Master of everything, slave of sex." Ramakrishna, the great spiritual giant, saw what was actually happening in the world. Now the same story is being repeated in the world today. Ramakrishna tells a story about a man who had been hunting for a job for a long time. Nobody would offer the poor man a job. Finally he went to the manager of a small factory, for he had been told that this manager had a broad heart and would give him a job. But the manager said there was no vacancy. A few days later he asked again; still no vacancy. The poor man kept going back, and each time he was rejected. One day he told one of his friends how the manager had been constantly turning him away without a job. His friend said, "You are a fool. Why do you go to him? Today go to his mistress, and tomorrow you will get the job." The manager was a very wealthy and important man, but he had this weakness. So the poor man went to the mistress and cried out, "Mother, I have a big family and they are starving. Save me, save me. Please tell the manager to give me a job." She replied, "Don't worry, my child, tomorrow I shall settle it." On the following day the manager said to his English boss, "Here is a man who has great ability. In everything he will bring much credit to our factory." Shortly afterward the man was offered a high post there.

This is Ramakrishna's story. It is still applicable today. The world-atmosphere has not yet changed. But it is bound to be changed. Who will do it? It is we, the aspirants; we, the seekers of the infinite Light. God has given us this matchless, unique task. And we have to accept and fulfill it here on earth.

In the outer world one can be a slave only to one master, but in the inner world one is bound to be a slave to many masters. These masters are doubt, fear, anxiety, temptation, frustration, imperfection, limitation, bondage and death. Self-control can be achieved only if we stop deceiving ourselves. We are apt to say that the world is deserting us in and out of season. But if we are sincere and we go deep within, then we come to see, feel and realize that it is we who started this game of deception. We came from God. We could have continued our game in infinite Light. We could have retired at our journey's close in the same infinite Light. But we entered into ignorance and became enamored of it. We loved ignorance and it loved us. Finally, we started eating greedily the fruits of ignorance. The result has been self-destruction. It is we who have opened the door of deception within us. When the forces of ignorance see that the door is wide open, they enter into us, into the innermost recesses of our heart. How can we pull them out and push them aside? We can do it through aspiration, through our inner mounting flame. This flame will kindle the unlit forces in us, awaken the slumbering beings in us and inundate our life with the Light of the Golden Beyond. Aspiration is the answer.

Spiritual sickness is an impurity in our heart, and this sickness has only one medicine, devotion: devotion to the cause, devotion to the goal, devotion to the Inner Pilot.

Self-control. Self-control means self-giving to God. Let us play our part. Let us give what we have. God will play His part. He will give us what He has. What we have is teeming ignorance. What He has is infinite Light. Let us trade.

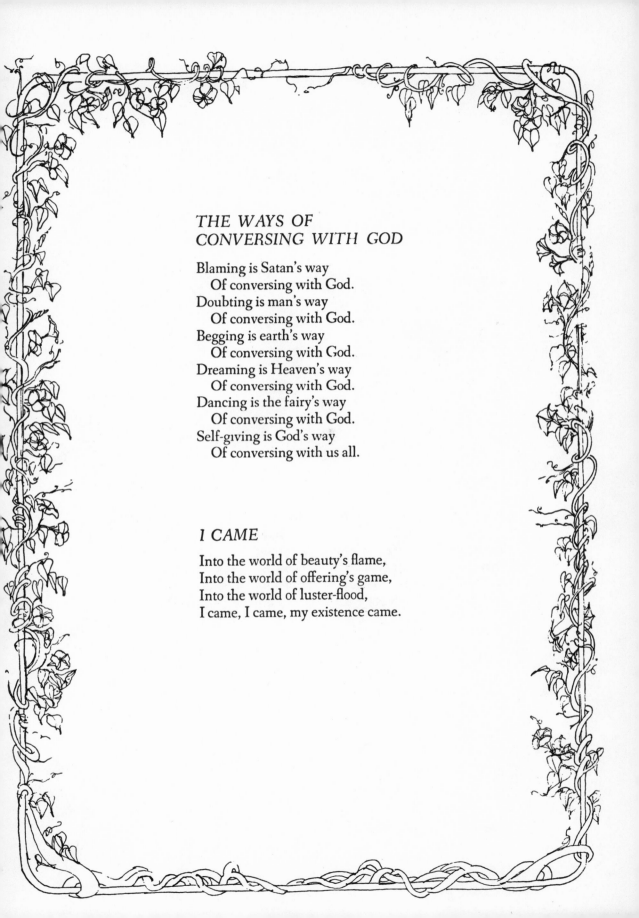

THE WAYS OF
CONVERSING WITH GOD

Blaming is Satan's way
   Of conversing with God.
Doubting is man's way
   Of conversing with God.
Begging is earth's way
   Of conversing with God.
Dreaming is Heaven's way
   Of conversing with God.
Dancing is the fairy's way
   Of conversing with God.
Self-giving is God's way
   Of conversing with us all.

I CAME

Into the world of beauty's flame,
Into the world of offering's game,
Into the world of luster-flood,
I came, I came, my existence came.

ATTACHMENT AND DETACHMENT

University of Toronto, Toronto, Canada
October 7, 1970

Attachment is my teacher:
"God lives in a cave,"
I learn.
Detachment is my teacher:
"God lives in a Palace,"
I learn.
Attachment demands my body's breath,
The life of the howling finite.
Detachment offers my soul's promise,
The Light of the Beckoning Beyond.

Attachment is the root of desire: ignorance is the root of attachment. In this world we are attached to the body, the mind, the vital and the heart. Why? Because we want to possess. Unfortunately, we forget that there is nothing on earth we can possess forever. No, not even for a long time. Take the body, for example. No matter how much attention we give it, this body lasts for only fifty, sixty or seventy years, and then it dies. We cannot possess even our own body forever. There is nothing on earth that we can possess forever if we are in the physical and crying for the fulfillment of the physical. But if we live in the soul, then we are living in the Eternal and for the External.

India's great philosopher Shankaracharya said, "Who is your wife, who is your son? This world is very peculiar. Brothers, think of the One who is eternally yours." This is the message of detachment. If you are attached to the physical person—the wife, the husband, the son, the friend—then you are only binding yourself and the other. But if you see the Object of adoration inside the wife, inside the husband, inside the son, then divine knowledge can dawn in you.

Lord Buddha left his beautiful wife and his little child when they were asleep. Before departing he said, "I loved you. I still love you. But I have to love the entire world also. Only if I can love the entire world will my love for you be complete." His human attachment had to surrender to the Divine Love in him. While they were leaving the kingdom, Buddha's charioteer asked him a significant question: "Are you not mean? How is it that you are leaving behind your wife who has been so affectionate to you? You are her treasure; you are her peerless wealth." The Buddha said, "You are mistaken. My wife's affection was binding me, and my affection was binding her. Now I am entering into the world at large where there is no one to bind me, and where I will not bind anyone. I am going to free myself and others."

At the root of all attachment is ignorance. Is ignorance invincible? The philosopher Aldous Huxley once said, "Ignorance is vincible. We don't want to know something; that is why we don't know it." He is absolutely right. Ignorance is not something permanent and unchangeable. We can enter into the very breath of ignorance and transform it into wisdom and knowledge. But instead, we deny the existence of the ignorance inside us. This is a mistake. We have to accept the fact that right now we are full of ignorance. That does not mean that we have no light within us. Deep inside there is a little light, but we have to bring this light to the fore and make it grow in order to realize our own highest Truth.

A real philosopher is one who is detached. He alone can have the vision of Truth. Once he has this vision, he can easily be indifferent to success and failure, joy and sorrow, pleasure and pain. His detachment does not mean that he will not help the world or receive help from it. It means he will not be bound to those he is helping or to those who are helping him. If we are attached, we are frustrated; but if we are detached, we are fulfilled. If we can feel that it is God who is operating in us and through us, as well as in and through the world, then we can be truly free.

It is said that before marriage a man is a woman's aspiration and after marriage he is a woman's exasperation. But what is the woman aspiring for? She is aspiring for the fulfillment of desire. When the object of desire is attained, disappointment and frustration reign. When we fulfill any desire of ours, we will find that we are not eating the delicious fruit that we expected, but rather some destructive, poisonous fruit.

In India there is a proverb that whoever has eaten the Delhi *ka laddu* (sweet cake of Delhi) feels disgusted, and whoever has not yet eaten it feels denied. That is always the case with desire fulfilled and desire unfulfilled. Fulfillment may follow desire, but it will not be the fulfillment that energizes you and gives you greater inner strength to do the right things. On the contrary, it will only destroy what little aspiration you already have.

Attachment does not diminish with age. Only through aspiration can we conquer attachment. In order to be free from attachment, we have to go through several stages. We have to study the scriptures and religious and spiritual books. We have to associate with spiritual aspirants who have studied these books and are now crying for the real light, or with those who have already gotten some light, insignificant or considerable, in their life of aspiration. We have to see and feel that in the ordinary world all around us is temptation, that at any moment we may fall victim to it, and that we must valiantly fight against it. We have to take our minds away from the physical consciousness and bodily demands. We have to enter into the world of expanded consciousness. We have to feel the necessity of attaining the divine Goal. We have to follow the guidance of our Inner Pilot, who is God, either in the form of a God-realized spiritual Master or in His own unembodied Form.

> To love those who love us is to do the right thing.
> To love those who do not love us is to do the nice thing.
> To love God who always loves us is to do the wise thing.
> When we do the right thing, we are free.
> When we do the nice thing, we are safe.
> When we do the wise thing, we are fulfilled.

ATTACHMENT

O seeker,
   You want to know
      What attachment is.
Attachment is when
   You love one
And do not love all.
Attachment is when
   You feel
That God has appointed only you
   To fulfill His Vision,
And not others.
Attachment is when
   You think
Of the creation first
     And
Not the Creator.
Attachment is when
    The spirit of bargain
      Haunts you
        Powerfully
        And
        Triumphantly.

PERFECTION

University of Ottawa, Ottawa, Canada
October 8, 1970

Perfection is what I have inherited from God in my inner life. Transformation is what I have inherited from God in my outer life.

What is perfection? Perfection is realization. Perfection is manifestation. Perfection in the inner world means realization. Perfection in the outer world means manifestation. A seeker is a fusion of individuality and personality. When a seeker carries his selfless individuality into the highest Vision of Reality and offers his all-loving personality to the Absolute Beyond, he achieves perfection in the world of Infinity's Eternity.

Some people say that perfection exists neither in heaven nor on earth. I cannot see eye to eye with them. Perfection does exist both in heaven and on earth. The very cry of earth is perfection. The very smile of heaven is perfection. Earth's soulful cry and heaven's glowing smile must go together. Then only will satisfaction dawn on God's Face. God can have satisfaction only when earth's cry and heaven's smile run together. When earth cries we must not think that earth is inferior to heaven, and when heaven smiles we must not think that heaven is superior to earth. No, it is not so. It is God, the growing man, who cries in and through earth to realize all that he can eventually be. And it is again God, the fulfilled man, who smiles in and through heaven in realizing what he already is.

Perfection is an impossibility: this is what today tells us. But tomorrow will tell us that perfection is an inevitability. There is always some time lapse between the planting of a seed and the harvest. In the spiritual life, the seed is aspiration and the harvest is realization. Without aspiration, realization can never dawn. What is aspiration? Is it something that we already have, or is it something we are going to have? It is both. If we say that we have aspiration, we are right because we do think of God and meditate on God at times. If we say that we do not yet have aspiration but are someday going to have it, we are also right, because our love for God is neither spontaneous nor constant. When we sit at the feet of Eternity we realize that aspiration is bound to be followed by realization. And after we have made friends with eternal time, we come to understand that realization was always there, hidden in our aspiration.

Perfection means living, spontaneous, constant oneness with the Inner Pilot. If we have a free access to the inner life, then perfection is our very soul and at the same time our only Goal. Now, why is it that we are still imperfect? We are imperfect precisely because we do not consciously cry for perfection in ourselves. We demand, or at least expect, infinitely more perfection in others than in ourselves. He and she are imperfect and I am trying to perfect them, we say. But is it not absurd on my part to criticize and try to perfect others when I myself am imperfect? In this we make a Himalayan blunder. If we are sincere enough, we will realize that we spend too much time thinking of others. It is good to think of others, but not with our criticizing, jealous, unlit mind. If we think of others with our soul's light, our soul's oneness, then automatically we are running toward perfection.

Let us think of perfecting ourselves, and while thinking of ourselves let us include the entire universe, or embody the entire universe in ourselves. Then we do not have to think of each individual on earth, for all are inside us. When I meditate, my entire body meditates with me. I do not have to think of my internal organs; they are inside me, meditating and aspiring with me. Similarly, during your concentration, meditation and contemplation, if you can feel that the entire universe is within you and that you are running toward your Goal, then the universe in totality will run with you.

We are all aspirants, seekers of the Infinite Truth, Light and Bliss. If we do not achieve perfection in our inner and outer life, who else can achieve perfection? It is we, the seekers of the Infinite, who have to embody, realize, reveal and manifest perfection. At every moment of our earthly existence, in fleeting time and in eternal Time, we have to embody the message of perfection. If we feel that the eternal Time is somewhere else and that only the fleeting time is at our disposal, we are mistaken. If we live in the body, we are making friends with fleeting time. If we live in the soul, we are making friends with eternal time. Since we are in the body, let us try to bring down the highest perfection from above into the body. If we can live in the soul even while in the body, let us reveal our already achieved perfection to the world at large.

My imperfect gift to God is yesterday, yesterday's experience. God's perfect gift to me is today, today's realization.

THEY ARE ONE

Truth and God are one,
God and Love are one.
Love and life are one,
Life and cry are one.
Cry and height are one,
Height and progress are one.
Progress and delight are one,
Delight and perfection are one.

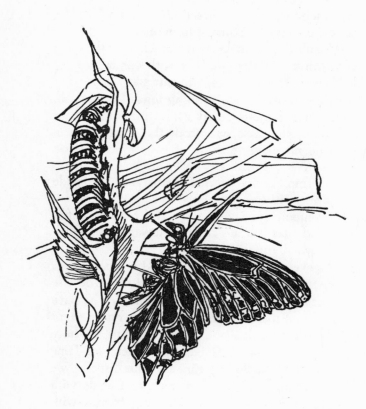

MORE IS NEEDED

Intention is good,
    But
Something more is needed.
And what is that thing?
    Action.
Action is good,
    But
Something more is needed.
And what is that thing?
    Realization.
Realization is good,
    But
Something more is needed.
And what is that thing?
    Perfection.

INSPIRATION, ASPIRATION
AND REALIZATION

McGill University, Montreal, Canada
October 9, 1970

What do we mean when we say "inspiration," "aspiration" and "realization"? Inspiration is the beginning of our spiritual journey; aspiration is the middle of our spiritual journey; and realization is the end of our spiritual journey. When we are inspired, we wish to see the Face of God. When we aspire, we eventually come to see the Face of God. When we realize, we grow into the very Image of God.

Arise, awake! This path is arduous. So we learn from the wise, and we have to follow in the footsteps of the wise. The path of spirituality is not a bed of roses. But neither is it a chimerical mist. The Golden Shores of the Beyond are not a mere promise. The crown of human aspiration is bound to be fulfilled on the Golden Shores of the Beyond.

Arise, awake! Here we must not stop. We have to walk, march, run, dive and fly. The moment we arise from our slumber, we see and feel the need for God in our human life, in our outer and inner life. When we wake up we see that not only do we need God, but God also needs us. Why? We need God to realize our highest, the ultimate transcendental Height. God needs us for His Self-Manifestation here on earth, His Manifestation in us and through us. When we walk along the path of spirituality, we see that God is already inside us. When we march, we see God marching beside us. When we run, we see that God is running in and through us. When we dive deep within, we see the peerless treasure waiting for us. When we fly, we see that we are flying in the welkin of the infinite Peace, Light and Bliss of the Beyond.

In the spiritual life everybody wants to realize God. But when it is a matter of aspiration, dedication, renunciation and surrender to the Will of the Inner Pilot, very few people are prepared to undergo the spiritual discipline. Everybody wants to realize God overnight; everybody wants to become the highest possible preceptor or Guru without going through the spiritual discipline of inspiration and aspiration.

It is like this. A seeker comes to a spiritual institution. The head of the institution asks him, "What do you want?" The seeker says, "I want to join your spiritual institution. Please give me some work." The head of the institution says, "There are only two kinds of work available here. Either you have to play the role of the disciple, or you have to play the role of the Guru or Master. You have to listen to the Guru, or you have to be the Guru and make others listen to you." The seeker immediately says, "Please, I want to play the role of the Guru." This is what actually happens in our spiritual life. Very often, when a seeker comes to the Master, he unconsciously thinks that he can also be a Master overnight. But I wish to say that it is not possible to become a spiritual giant or to achieve self-discovery or to realize God overnight. It takes time. Here most of you are students. You know how many years it takes to get your Master's degree—fifteen or twenty years. To acquire spiritual knowledge also demands many years of study. This study has to be undertaken before one becomes a spiritual Master.

We are all living in a world of duality, multiplicity and variety. When we want to elevate our consciousness to the Highest and try to aspire, desire, the thief, robs us. He takes away our psychic aspiration, our pure devotion toward God, our surrendering will which we offer to the Almighty Will. The Christ said, "Except a man be born again, he cannot see the Kingdom of God." What do we learn from this lofty message? We learn that the life of desire has to give way to the life of aspiration. If the life of aspiration does not come to the fore, then a new life can never dawn. The Kingdom of God can be established only when we kindle the flame of aspiration deep within us.

Every day we are facing the ideal and the real. Our ideal is God, but the reality that we are facing is something totally different: ignorance. We are caught in the meshes of ignorance. The ideal and the real must go together. God is the Ideal; God is also the Real. We make solemn promises every day. We say that our ideal is to raise our consciousness to the Highest, our ideal is to achieve perfect Perfection. But when we face the real within us and without, we see that we are imperfection incarnate. Why? Because we are wanting in aspiration. We are wallowing in the pleasures of desires. Naturally, aspiration cannot play a proper role in us.

There are two Sanskrit words, *abhyasa* and *tyaga*. *Abhyasa* means practice and *tyaga* means renunciation. Every day we have to practice the inner life. When we practice meditation for fifteen minutes, God practices Compassion. We offer Him our heart's soulful cry, and in His own way He offers us His boundless, infinite Compassion. This is what we and God both practice. Now, renunciation. What are we going to renounce? The world? Society? Humanity? No! We are going to renounce our imperfections, bondage and death. When we go deep within, we see that we do not actually renounce these negative qualities of ours. Rather, we transform them. If imperfection looms large and important in our life, then we try to perfect our imperfection with our conscious awareness of Light. If we notice bondage within us, then we try to transform our bondage into freedom. If death is constantly knocking at our door, which it always is, we try to transform our death into Immortality.

Earlier, I spoke about the need for aspiration to realize God. But inspiration is also necessary. Why do we need inspiration? Can we not immediately achieve realization without first going through inspiration? Let us take an example. An artist creates a painting. If he is not inspired, his creation will have no meaning, or significance. It will be a mechanical creation; it will be wanting in life. I wish to say that on the strength of his inspiration, the artist gives life to a portrait. When people see and appreciate the portrait, their appreciation takes the form of an offering of their own life. The portrait gets new life from the admirers. And when a spiritual person looks at the picture, he offers it divine life. So first we see the artist's creation, then we see the admirers' creation and finally we see the Master's creation, which offers divine life to the picture.

When a man walks along the path of spirituality, his inspiration is the awakening life that he offers to himself. When he aspires, his aspiration is the illumining life that he offers to himself. And when he becomes a realized person, he offers the Life Divine, the Life of Immortality, to his awakened and illumined life.

What is realization? When we use the term "realization" in our spiritual life, people are very often confused. They feel that a realized person is totally different from an ordinary person, that he behaves in a very unusual way. But I wish to say that a realized person need not and should not behave in an unusual way. What has he realized? The ultimate Truth in God. And who is God? God is someone or something absolutely natural.

When a man realizes the highest Truth, he tries to offer the highest Truth to humanity at large. Most often unrealized people or unspiritual people think that a realized person, if he is truly realized, has to perform miracles at every moment. Miracles and God-Realization need not and should not go together. When you stand in front of a spiritual Master, what you expect to see and what you do see is Peace, Light, Bliss and divine Power. Now, where does he hold this power? Not in his arms or legs, or in his head, but deep inside the inmost recesses of his heart. Enter into him and you are bound to feel infinite Peace, infinite Light and infinite Bliss. But if you expect something else from a realized soul, if you come to a spiritual Master thinking that because he has realized the highest he can fulfill your teeming desires, make you a multimillionaire in the twinkling of an eye, you are totally mistaken. These are the kinds of things he does not do. If it is the Will of the Supreme, the Master can easily make someone a multimillionaire overnight. He can bring down material prosperity in abundant measure, but this is not the Will of the Supreme. What you can expect from a Master and from a Master's realization is Peace, Light and Bliss.

REALIZATION

Realization,
What is it?
It is nothing other than illusion.
For whom?
For him who wants to govern the world.
Realization,
What is it?
It is nothing other than satisfaction.
For whom?
For him who wants to serve the world.

I CHALLENGED THE INVISIBLE

I drove the chariot of the sun
Athwart the arch of blue-gold Heaven,
Dissolving the negative intruders,
        Fear and doubt,
Embracing the positive prompters,
        Faith and Love.
Thousands of years ago
I challenged the invisible.
At long last, today
My challenge has been accepted.
Enlightenment fondly braves
The untiring searcher.

MY SONGS

My desire-song
   Began.
But I do not know
  When I stopped it.
My aspiration-song
   Began.
But I do not know
  How it began
   Or
  How I am
Continuing it.
My realization-song
   Began.
Who began it? God.
Who continues it? God.
Who listens to it? God.
Who is enamored of it? God.

INVOCATION

Supreme, Supreme, Supreme, Supreme!
  I bow to Thee, I bow.
  My life Thy golden plow;
My journey's Goal Thy soulful Dream.
Supreme, Supreme, Supreme, Supreme!
  I bow to Thee, I bow.

Supreme, I am Thy glowing Grace.
  My world Thy Feet of Light,
  My breath Thy Vision's kite.
Thou art one Truth, one Life, one Face.
Supreme, Supreme, Supreme, Supreme!
  I bow to Thee, I bow.

MY ROSE PETALS

IS DEATH THE END?

University of Kent, Canterbury, England
November 9, 1970

Death is not the end. Death can never be the end. Death is the road. Life is the traveler. The soul is the guide.

When the traveler is tired and exhausted, the guide instructs the traveler to take either a short or a long rest, and then the traveler's journey begins again.

In the spiritual life, when an aspirant does not cry for a higher light, bliss and power, it is the birth of his death.

In the ordinary life, when an unaspiring man wallows in the mire of ignorance, it is the real victory of death.

What can we learn from the inner life which desires the extinction of death? The inner life tells us that life is soulfully precious, that time is fruitfully precious.

Life without the aspiration of time is meaningless.

Time without the aspiration of life is useless.

Our mind thinks of death. Our heart thinks of life. Our soul thinks of immortality. Mind and death can be transcended. Heart and life can be expanded. Soul and immortality can be fulfilled.

When the mind and death are transcended, man will have a new home: Light, the Light of the Beyond.

When the soul and immortality are fulfilled, man will have a new goal: Delight, the transcendental Delight.

Today man feels that death is an unavoidable necessity.

Tomorrow man will feel that immortality is an unmistakable reality.

Unfortunately, most of us cherish wrong conceptions about death. We think death is something unusual, something destructive. But we have to know that right now death is something natural, normal and, to some extent, inevitable.

Lord Krishna tells Arjuna, "O Arjuna, certain is death for the born and certain is birth for the dead. Therefore what is inevitable ought not to be a cause for thy sorrow."

The Chandogya Upanishad tells us something significant: "When the hour of death approaches [that is to say, in the final hour], what should we do? We should take refuge in three sublime thoughts: we are indestructible; we can never be shaken; we are the very essence of life."

When the hour of death approaches us, if we feel that we can never be destroyed, that nothing can shake us and that we are the very essence of life, then where is sorrow, where is fear, where is death? No death.

Sarada Devi, the consort of Sri Ramakrishna, said something very significant: "The difference between a spiritual man and an ordinary man is very simple. Easily you can know the difference between the two. An ordinary man cries and sheds bitter tears when death approaches him; whereas a spiritual man, if he is really spiritual, will laugh and laugh when death approaches, for to him death is fun, nothing else."

Here we have to say that a spiritual man enters into the cosmic game; he becomes a conscious instrument of the cosmic game. That is why he knows that death is not an extinction. It is only a short or a long rest.

Again and again we shall have to come back into the world. We have to work for God here on earth. There is no escape. We have to realize the Highest here on earth. We have to fulfill the Highest on earth. God will not allow us to waste or squander the potentialities and possibilities of the soul. Impossible.

Kipling's immortal utterance runs:

> They will come back, come back again,
> As long as the red Earth rolls.
> He never wasted a leaf or a tree.
> Do you think He would squander souls?

Each incarnation is leading us toward a higher life, a better life. We are in the process of evolution. Each incarnation is a rung in the ladder of evolution. Man is progressing consciously and unconsciously. But if he makes progress in each incarnation consciously, then he is expediting his spiritual progress. Realization will take place much sooner for him than for those who are making progress unconsciously.

We know that we started our journey from the mineral life and then entered into the plant life. Then we entered into the animal kingdom. From there we have come into the human world. But here is not the end. We have to grow into divine beings. Unless and until we have become divinized and transformed, God will not be satisfied with us. He can manifest in us and through us only when we are totally transformed and fully illumined. So when we think of our evolution—inner evolution and outer evolution—we get abundant joy. We lose nothing, nothing, in so-called death.

Jalalu'd-din Rumi most beautifully and soulfully tells us about evolution:

> A stone I died and rose again a plant,
> A plant I died and rose an animal;
> I died an animal and was born a man.
> Why should I fear? What have I lost by death?

What is death after all? Death is a sleeping child. And what is life? Life is a child that is playing, singing and dancing at every moment before the Father.

Death is the sleeping child inside the heart of the Inner Pilot. Life is inspiration. Life is aspiration. Life is realization. Life is not the reasoning mind. Life is not the intellectual mind. Life is not a game of frustration. No.

Life is the message of divinity on earth. Life is God's conscious channel to fulfill divinity in humanity on earth.

There is much truth in Confucius' saying: "We don't know life. How can we know death?"

Now I wish to say that we can know life. If we realize life as God's embodiment of Truth, Light, Peace and Bliss, then we know what life truly is and recognize death as nothing but a rest—one necessary at the present stage of evolution.

There will come a time when rest will not be necessary at all. Only Life will reign supreme—the Life of the Beyond, the Life of the ever-transcending Beyond. This Life is not and cannot be the sole monopoly of an individual, no. Each human being is to be flooded with this Life of the ever-transcending Beyond, for it is here in this Life Divine that God will manifest Himself unreservedly—here, here on earth.

DEATH

Death, how often do you speak to God?
"I speak to God constantly."
Can you tell me
What both of you talk about?
"We talk about our achievements
            And
Our disappointments.
I tell Him about my achievements
            On earth
And my disappointments in heaven.
God tells me about His achievements
            In heaven
And His disappointments on earth."
I see.
Thank you, Death.

THE UNDIVINE AND THE DIVINE

The undivine flourish,
The divine die young:
This is what we hear,
This is what we think,
This is what we know.
My soul wants to add
Something to this lofty theory:
The undivine flourish
In the closed coffin of Death.
The divine die young
In the Lap of Immortality.

DEATH HAS APPROACHED OUR DOOR

Death has approached our door. We tell death
    to go away.
We tell death we sing the song of the Lord Supreme.
Here on earth we shall live, and divinely awakened
    we shall remain on earth.
We worshipers of Light,
We lovers of Fire, shall destroy the thunder of
    death in the ocean of Infinite Fulfillment.
Death has approached our door today.

THE END OF ALL KNOWLEDGE

University of Nottingham, Nottingham, England
November 10, 1970

Aum. Purnam adah, purnam idam, purnat purnam udacyate. Purnasya purnam adaya purnam evavasisyate. "Infinity is that. Infinity is this. From Infinity, Infinity has come into existence. From Infinity, when Infinity is taken away, Infinity remains."

The end of all knowledge. The end of all knowledge is God-Knowledge. This knowledge tells man what he can eventually be. This knowledge tells man that he can have a conscious and inseparable oneness with God.

Here at this point the Son of God tells us, "I and my Father are one." On the strength of his highest realization and inseparable oneness with his Father, he says, "I and my Father are one."

God-Knowledge tells us not only that God is within us and for us, but also that each human being is of Him. Finally, this God-Knowledge tells us that each human being has to become God Himself.

Brahmasmi . . . "I am the Brahman. I am God." This is what we have learned from the Vedic seers of yore. The Vedic seers realized the Supreme Truth and then offered the Supreme Truth to mankind. Today's man—today's unrealized, unfulfilled man—is tomorrow's realized and fulfilled God.

The end of human knowledge is the beginning of divine knowledge. Divine knowledge and human ignorance: these are two things we see in our day-to-day life. Divine knowledge is an illumining, fulfilling and immortalizing power. Human ignorance is a mad elephant, a destructive power. Divine knowledge is the very birth of immortality. Human ignorance is the song of death.

I am sure most of you are well acquainted with our Upanishads. There is an Upanishad called Kanshitaki Upanishad. Unfortunately, this Upanishad is not well known. This Upanishad, which offers a sublime knowledge, says:

> Speech is not what one should desire to understand. One should know the speaker. . . .
> The deed is not what one should desire to understand. One should know the doer. . . .
> Mind is not what one should desire to understand. One should know the thinker.

Here at this point I wish to say that, from the spiritual point of view, Peace, Light, Bliss and Power are not what one should desire to understand. Rather, one should seek to know the living embodiment of Peace, Light, Bliss and Power. It is He who can bring to the fore these divine qualities in sincere, aspiring souls. It is He who has the capacity to inspire the seekers. At the same time, it is He who is of considerable help in awakening the slumbering consciousness of human souls. And, finally, it is He who expedites the seekers' journey.

The end of all knowledge is self-knowledge. "Know thyself," which all of you are familiar with. The Sanskrit term for it is *Atmanam viddhi.* Know thyself. How can we know ourselves? We have to know ourselves by accepting help from someone who already knows himself. He is our teacher. He is more like our private tutor than a schoolteacher. A schoolteacher is entitled to examine us, to pass or fail us, but this private tutor helps us pass the examination. He wholeheartedly teaches us. So a spiritual teacher is a private tutor and not a schoolteacher.

Self-knowledge is self-discovery, and in self-discovery we feel the conquest of our own self. Self-discovery, God-Knowledge and self-conquest: these are one and the same.

The Welsh Triad says, "There are three kinds of men: man in man, who does good for good and evil for evil; man in God, who does good for evil; and man in the devil, who does evil for good."

In our spiritual life, we have one more category: the man of God, the messenger of God, the representative of God, the channel of God, the instrument of God. This instrument of God constantly feels that he is not the doer but a mere instrument.

Lord Sri Krishna in the *Bhagavad-Gita,* the Song Celestial, tells his dearest friend and disciple, Arjuna, *Nimitta matram bhava savyasachin,* "You just become an instrument."

So the man of God feels in the inmost recesses of his heart that he is a mere instrument. He works for God; he lives for God. He feels that God-Realization is not enough. He feels that God-Manifestation here on earth is of paramount importance.

Many have realized the Highest, the transcendental Truth. But there are few who cry for the perfection of humanity. There are very few who try to change the face of the world. The chosen instruments of God want to manifest God here on earth. They do not care much for earthly good or evil. They transcend the so-called good and evil. They care only for God's inner dictates. Constantly they listen to the dictates of their Inner Pilot; and then, on the strength of their inseparable oneness with their Inner Pilot, they offer their selfless, dedicated service to humanity. They try to offer knowledge, divine knowledge, to aspiring humanity. Again, they tell humanity that God-Realization is not their sole monopoly.

Everybody has to realize God, the transcendental Truth. Everybody is destined to realize the highest Truth, but he who cries for the inner light will naturally reach the goal sooner than the one who is still fast asleep.

The great Savior has taught us, "No man can serve two masters." Here we have two masters: ignorance and knowledge. Now, if we want to wallow in the pleasures and mire of ignorance, we are serving ignorance the master. Again, it is we who have the opportunity to serve the other master, knowledge, the light. If we aspire, then our master is knowledge and knowledge-light. If we want to serve our master, knowledge-light, then the message of realization, the message of perfection, can never remain a far cry.

The immortal poet George Eliot sings, "Our deeds still travel with us from afar, and what we have been makes us what we are."

From the spiritual point of view, what do we learn from this soulful message? We come to learn that we have been victims to teeming desires and here is the result: we are still earthbound. We are bound by the fetters of ignorance; we are caught. We want to possess the world. To our widest surprise and sorrow, we are already caught; we are already possessed.

Now again, it is we who have the capacity, potentiality and opportunity to free ourselves from the mire of ignorance. If we aspire today, tomorrow we shall grow into a divine reality; and in that divine reality our realization will loom large.

We have to know at every moment that we have to be true to ourselves. Do we want Light? Do we want Perfection? Or out of curiosity do we want to have just an iota of Light and Truth? Unless and until we are true to ourselves, true to our inner quest, we can never, never see the face of reality, fulfillment and perfection.

Most of you know that the immortal poet Shakespeare, in *Hamlet,* says, "This above all: to thine own self be true, and it shall follow, as the night the day, thou canst not then be false to any man."

If we really want the inner light, if we really have the inner cry to see God face to face, there can be nothing either on earth or in heaven to deny us, to deny our soul's inmost quest. Each individual being has limited freedom. This freedom can be utilized either to aspire or to desire. If we desire, the teeming clouds will undoubtedly eclipse our Knowledge-sun. If we aspire, God, the Inner Pilot, will inspire us to run fast, faster, fastest toward the Destined Goal, the Goal of the Beyond.

When we enter into the spiritual life, we come to realize that there is no end to our journey. Today we may think that this is the goal we have been crying for. But when we go deep within, we feel that today's goal is tomorrow's starting point.

God is in everything. We have to see God in everything, feel God in everything, in every human being. But that is not enough. We have to see, feel, realize; then we have to go one step further. We have to realize that there is no end to our realization. Every moment we have to feel that, on the strength of our highest realization, we are running toward the ever-transcending Beyond.

The end of all knowledge is God-Knowledge. We have to see God. This is the ultimate knowledge. Now, there are three ways to see God. One way is to see God through a window. This we can do if we concentrate daily, say for six hours, on God. If we want to see God through an open door, we have to meditate. We have to meditate daily for at least twelve hours. But if we want to see God face to face, as you are seeing me and I am seeing you, then we have to meditate twenty-four hours a day.

To see God constantly face to face is the beginning and blossoming of the Transcendental Knowledge.

ONE FACT FOR ALL,
ONE WISDOM FOR ALL

One fact for all:
   All human beings are weak.
One fact for all:
   All human beings are uncertain.
One fact for all:
   All human beings are imperfect.
One wisdom for all:
   God is Light.
One wisdom for all:
   God's Hour is for all.
One wisdom for all:
   God is the slave of His own Compassion.

HIS KNOWLEDGE AND
HIS UNDERSTANDING

He knows everything.
He knows everything
   And understands nothing.
He understands everything.
He understands everything
   And knows nothing.
To be in the world of the soul
   Is to know everything.
To be in the world of the mind
   Is to understand nothing.
To be in the world of the vital
   Is to understand everything.
To be in the world of the body
   Is to know nothing.

PERFECTION-GOAL

University of London, London, England
November 11, 1970

Perfection is the seeker's fulfilling realization and fulfilled manifestation. Everything else has dawned on earth save perfection, perfect Perfection.

Perfection is the tree.

Perfect Perfection is the fruit.

Man's speculation about perfection is his ignorance. Man's concentration on perfection is his knowledge. Man's meditation on perfection is his wisdom. Man's contemplation on perfection is his world-illumining, world-transforming inner eye.

> God's Message is Perfection.
> Man's message is temptation.
> God's Message is Perfection.
> Man's message is frustration.
> God's Message is Perfection.
> Man's message is destruction.

Perfection-Goal and the freedom-soul go together. He who reaches the state of freedom-soul has conquered his inner life and immortalized his outer life. He is the chosen instrument of God. He is the direct channel of God. He is the representative of God here on earth.

Cry and try.

When we cry to see the transcendental Light and when we try to perfect our outer nature, our perfection does not remain a far cry. Perfection is ours.

Exert and control.

When we exert the divine in us and control the animal in us, perfection begins to dawn within us. The flower of perfection blooms.

See and be.

When we try to see the truth with the Eye of God, not with our own eyes, and when we consciously try to be the surrendered instrument of God, perfection in no time dawns. The Golden All of perfection beckons our aspiring hearts. It is true that perfection cannot be achieved overnight. Realization cannot be achieved all at once. It takes time.

Let me tell you a story. A young seeker once came up to a spiritual Master for initiation, and was duly initiated. Then the following day he said, "Master, now that you have initiated me, you have to give me realization. I want to see God."

The Master said, "My child, how is it possible for you to realize God in one day?"

Two days later, he said, "Oh, I want to realize God."

The Master said, "You are not ready."

A few days later, again the same request: "Master, I want to realize God." He had not completed his task. He had not launched into the spiritual path properly. Just the other day the Master had initiated him, but now he was crying for realization without following the proper method. Without swimming in the sea of aspiration, he wanted to realize God.

On his way to the Ganges for a dip, the Master invited this particular disciple to come with him. As the two entered the water, the Master pressed the disciple's head underwater for a couple of minutes. When he released it, the Master asked, "What did you feel when I was pressing your head into the water?"

"Master, I was gasping for air. I was practically dying and I thought I would not survive. The moment you released me, I got my life back."

The Master said, "If you can come to that same state of consciousness and feel that without God you cannot live even for a few minutes, you will realize God. You will realize God at that moment on the strength of your highest aspiration. Your inmost inner flame has to be kindled, and then you have to cry—cry for God as a child cries for his mother. Only then is God-Realization possible."

The disciple learned the lesson. Truly and soulfully he entered into the spiritual life and listened to all his Master's dictates. Wholeheartedly he launched into the spiritual life. He felt the necessity of freedom from the domain of desires. He felt the necessity to grow into the mounting flame of aspiration, constant aspiration. Then realization for him was not a far cry. He did realize God.

When we use the term *heaven*, we feel that heaven is all light, delight and perfection. But where is that heaven? It is deep within us, in the inmost recesses of our hearts. High heaven, higher heaven and highest heaven are all within us.

When we offer our soulful thoughts to our brothers and sisters, we live in high heaven.

When we offer the results of our soulful actions to mankind, we live in higher heaven.

Finally, when we offer our soulful existence to humanity at large, unreservedly and unconditionally, we live in the highest heaven.

We can live in the highest heaven every day. God has given us the capacity. He has given us the potentiality. It is we who have to manifest our inner potentiality and capacity. We are all surcharged with indomitable inner courage. Unfortunately, we do not use our inner unlimited capacity. We use our outer limited capacity. We are afraid of diving deep within. Inside is the treasure. Inside is the key. We do not know where we have put the key. We have totally forgotten. We do not know where the treasure lies.

At this point we see the need for a spiritual Master who knows where the key is and where the treasure lies. He does not give something of his own to the seeker. He only brings to the fore the seeker's inner wealth. God-Realization is not his sole monopoly. Everybody will realize God, without fail. It is a matter of time. One realizes God today on the strength of his inner inspiration. Another realizes God tomorrow on the strength of his sincere aspiration. Everybody will realize God at God's choice hour. Again, those of us who are sincere seekers can expedite our journey. We can walk toward our goal. We can march toward our goal. We can run toward our goal. If we run, naturally we shall reach the goal sooner than those who are walking toward their destination.

Perfection-Goal. Perfect Perfection here on earth has to be manifested, but how? We have to start our journey with inspiration. We have to feel every day deep within us in all our activities the necessity of inspiration. Without inspiration there can be no proper achievement. Then we have to go one step further. After inspiration we have to feel the momentous necessity of aspiration. Inspiration is not all. We have to aspire to reach the Golden All, to see the Golden Shores of the Beyond, the ever-transcending Beyond. This is what we expect from aspiration, the mounting flame within us.

But aspiration is not enough, either. We have to meditate. Aspiration includes meditation. When we meditate, we have to feel that we are entering into Infinity, Eternity and Immortality. These are not vague terms, but our true possessions. To someday enter into our own divine possessions—Infinity, Eternity and Immortality—is our birthright.

Then, when we become advanced in our meditation, when meditation starts offering us its fruit, we enter the realm of realization. We realize the highest Truth in this body, here on earth. We do not have to go elsewhere to realize God. We do not have to enter a Himalayan cave or sit on a snowcapped mountain in order to practice spirituality. No. Here on earth, in the hustle and bustle of life, we have to practice spirituality. We have to accept earth as it stands, as it is. If we are afraid of earth, if we shy away from earth, then God-Realization will always remain a far cry. Here on earth we have to realize the highest Truth.

But even realization is not enough. After realization we have to reveal our realization. If we do not reveal our realization, we act like a miser, hoarding our treasure. This is not right. We have to offer our realization in the form of revelation to mankind.

Yet revelation is not enough, either. We have to enter into the domain of manifestation. If we do not manifest what we have realized here on earth, if Mother Earth does not receive the fruit of our realization, and if She does not have it for good, we can never be truly fulfilled. Mother Earth has to be fed with the fruit of our realization. Here on earth the manifestation of realization has to take place; and when manifestation takes place, perfection is bound to dawn. Perfect Perfection is nothing other than the absolute manifestation of God's Transcendental Will here on earth.

We are all seekers of the Infinite Truth. It is our bounden duty to rise high, higher, highest. Each human being has come into the world with the message of perfection. No human being on earth will remain unrealized. No human being on earth will remain unfulfilled. No human being on earth will remain imperfect.

Realization, fulfillment and perfection: these are three brothers. Realization is the youngest, fulfillment is the middle, and perfect Perfection is the eldest in the family. These three brothers must go together. They have to walk along the field of aspiration. They have to swim in the sea of meditation. They have to fly in the sky, the blue welkin of contemplation.

God-Realization, God-Revelation and God-Manifestation can take place only when man feels that he has to transcend himself. His goal of today is not the ultimate Goal. Today's goal has to be transcended tomorrow. Today's goal is the foundation-stone. Every moment we have to transcend ourselves, and, while transcending, deep within us we shall cherish the message of perfection.

Perfection is bound to loom large and important in all our activities if we feel that aspiration is the only thing we need, the only thing we are striving for.

In aspiration lies the key that can ultimately open up the door of perfect Perfection.

WHEN I WAS BORN

When I was born
In the heart of my sun,
    I was my Duty's Role.
When I was born
In the heart of my moon,
    I was my Beauty's Soul.
When I was born
In the heart of my surrender-will,
    I was my Perfection-Goal.

IN MY HEART-DAWN AND SOUL-SUN

I loved my life's morning walks.
Hope-beauty led my eyes and guided my steps.
I love my life's midday runs.
Reality's naked life
Has sent uncertainty into destruction-exile.
I shall love my life's evening stumblings.
Life divine shall embrace the abyss of science.
Evening does not mark the end.
Evening is the precursor of a purer
Dawn and a brighter sun.
In my Heart-Dawn, my preparation shall begin.
In my Soul-Sun, my perfection shall bloom.

PRACTICE MAKES PERFECT

Practice makes perfect.
God believes in this theory;
   Therefore
He practiced Compassion.
Lo, He has become Compassion,
 Unconditional Compassion.
Practice makes perfect.
God believes in this theory;
   Therefore
He practiced surrender.
Lo, He has become perfect Surrender,
 Surrender to man's countless desires.

BOYS AND GIRLS

Boys will be boys;
Girls will be girls.
Boys will reach their Goal
Singing and running.
Girls will reach their Goal
Dancing and diving.
Boys will be boys;
Girls will be girls.
Boys will realize God,
The Highest Realization.
Girls will manifest God,
The Absolute Perfection.

HOW TO CONQUER FEAR

American College, Paris
November 13, 1970

Our body is limited; that is why the body has fear. Our vital is unconscious; that is why the vital has fear. Our mind is obscure; that is why the mind has fear. Our heart is unaspiring; that is why the heart has fear.

To free our body from fear, what we need is the glorious experience of our soul. To free our vital from fear, what we need is the dynamic and conscious expansion of our soul. To free our mind from fear, what we need is the transforming illumination of our soul. Finally, to free our heart from fear, what we need is the fulfilling perfection of our soul.

Man's fear does not allow him to see the face of reality, the ultimate Reality. Man's fear does not allow him to reach the Golden Shores of the Beyond. Man's fear does not allow him to fulfill God for God's sake.

But God, the Author of all good, has boundless Compassion, Concern and Love for mankind.

> God's Compassion saves man.
> God's Concern liberates man.
> God's Love fulfills man.

When we unconsciously think of fear or cherish fear, fear smilingly shakes hands with us. When we consciously think of fear or cherish fear, fear triumphantly embraces us. But when we unconsciously think of our inner courage, God cries with His divine Cry, for He feels that here He has a chosen instrument.

Now, earth is afraid of heaven's transcendental Light. Heaven is afraid of earth's abysmal ignorance. God says to earth, "My son, do not act like a fool. Heaven's transcendental Light is not going to blind you. Heaven's Light is not going to expose you. On the contrary, heaven's Light is going to illumine you. Heaven's Light is going to transform you."

God says to heaven, "Do not be a fool. Earth's abysmal ignorance cannot bind you. It cannot destroy you. On the contrary, earth's ignorance will be offered to you. It is you who will transform the face of earth."

God says, "I need both of you: heaven and earth.

"Heaven! The message of realization you will have to give to earth.

"Earth! The message of manifestation, My divine Manifestation, you will have to offer to heaven."

Fear comes from our deep-rooted ignorance. We do not see the light with our inner vision. We see the light with our outer, human, limited, earthbound understanding.

Let me tell you a short story. An old man walking along the street one evening came across a rope. There was no light, and he thought the rope was actually a snake. He was all fear, and let out a scream, running as fast as he could. While running he fell down and broke his leg. Some friends nearby heard him shouting and screaming, so they came with sticks. He was shouting all the time, thinking that there was a snake there. When his friends came they too thought that it was a snake. In the dark they started striking the rope, and unfortunately began hitting one another.

The shouting continued, and soon another party came with a light and discovered that it was just a piece of rope and not a snake. So when the light entered, they discovered that it was a rope and not a snake.

Similarly, in our human life, when light enters into our physical consciousness, every kind of fear is bound to disappear. We are wanting in light. That is why fear, at every moment, consciously and deliberately looms large in our life of desire and in our life of aspiration.

But if we are sincere enough to go deep within and feel that inner courage belongs to us, inner courage can dawn at every moment. It is more than willing to come to the fore. Bringing this inner courage to the fore is the conscious awakening of our inner being. Everyone has this inner being. But, unfortunately, very few of us want to feed it. We feed our body in order to strengthen ourselves. We study books to feed our minds. We do many things to energize our outer being, but we do practically nothing to feed our inner being.

It is in our inner existence that we can grow into an adamantine will; and when we use our adamantine will, which we can easily have at our behest, we can conquer the very breath of fear. Here on earth our inner adamantine and indomitable will can and will reign supreme. Only one thing we need: a conscious awareness of the Divine Light which is ours. It is our birthright to realize and fulfill this inner Light.

There can be no fear, there can't be even an iota of fear when we live in the effulgence of our soul. To live constantly in the divine effulgence of our soul only one thing is needed: a conscious inner cry. This inner cry is called aspiration, the mounting flame deep within us. When this flame rises up toward the highest, it illumines everything around it. Darkness is transformed into light, fear into strength, doubt into certainty, ignorance into wisdom, and death into immortality.

FEAR

Whom do I fear?
The Lord? The One?
Not true. I am
My Father's son.

What do I fear?
My ignorance vast—
The sleepless spear,
The eyeless dust.

Why do I fear?
Because my eyes
See not the Smile
Of the golden skies.

And what is fear?
A tempting call
From the bondage-sphere
Of an airtight ball.

And where is fear?
It is everywhere,
Death's atmosphere,
Shameless and bare.

NEVER

Never
He thinks out of fear;
Never
He fears to think.
Never
He loves out of fear;
Never
He fears to love.
Never
He becomes one out of fear;
Never
He fears to become one.
He thinks only of his life divine,
He fears only his ignorance,
He loves only his soul,
He becomes only his goal.

OCCULTISM

American Center for Arts, Paris
November 14, 1970

Occultism is a vast subject about which I could go on talking for hours and hours. But since time is limited, I wish to give only a short talk on occultism.

Occultism is an art. It is an inner art.

Occultism is a science. It is an outer science.

Occultism as an art awakens and inspires our inner life. Occultism as a science energizes and stimulates our outer life. A great occultist is a dynamic athlete. He fights against doubt. He fights against impurity. He fights against imperfection.

If you want to be an occultist, a divine athlete, then your life-boat has to ply between the shores of self-observation and self-correction in the river of emotion. That is to say, the human emotion has to be curbed, perfected. But the divine emotion has to be practiced, enlarged. This divine emotion makes us feel that we are in God, with God and for God. Human emotion, however, binds us, and with its help we try to bind others. Here we play the game of possession: to possess and be possessed. But the divine emotion is something else. Here we enlarge our consciousness, transforming our earthbound life into the infinite expanse of light.

An occultist has a universal mind. This mind is his watchtower. And he has an eye which we call the "third eye." Apart from our two eyes, we have a third eye which is located in between and slightly above the eyebrows. This eye is the eye of inner vision. This eye an occultist uses as a dynamic, successful and effective weapon.

An occultist has two names, an inner name and an outer name. His inner name is unwavering, unswerving Concentration. His outer name is Dynamic Revelation.

In our spiritual life we notice two brothers: occultism and spirituality. Occultism teaches us how to be brave and quick in the battle-field of life. Spirituality teaches us how to be pure and sure in all spheres and activities of life. Occultism wants to conquer time and space. Spirituality wants to conquer darkness and ignorance. When occultism wants to conquer time and space, it wants to do it in the twinkling of an eye. When spirituality wants to conquer darkness and ignorance, it does it at God's chosen hour.

An occultist has no time for idle daydreams, but he has all the time to see the face of willpower, adamantine willpower, within us. He has all the time to see victory's crown here on earth.

Now, there are various types of occultists, but we can put them into three major categories: an ordinary occultist, an occultist who is a little bit higher and an occultist who is of the highest order. An ordinary occultist will do many things contrary to the divine law, the divine dispensation. For name and fame he will do quite a few things which are damaging and destructive. I wish to tell you a story.

Once there were three occultists. One occultist lived near a restaurant. He didn't have enough money to buy anything, so every night he used to threaten the proprietor of the restaurant occultly. Using his occult power, he commanded him to send him, three times a day, the most delicious meals. This went on for months and years. The proprietor used to send meals three times a day to this occultist because he was being ruthlessly threatened at night.

The second occultist lived near a courthouse. Every day he would see hundreds of people coming in and out. He used to tell them what was happening in the farthest corners of the globe, leaving them all wonderstruck. And the following morning, the newspaper showed that everything the occultist said had been true.

Now, the third occultist lived near a church. Every day when the sincere seekers would go to the church, he would pray to the Lord Supreme to increase their aspiration, in order to expedite their salvation. Then, as they came out of the church after praying, he used to offer the same prayer to the Almighty: "O Father, I pray to You to give them illumination. With my occult power I wish to expedite their spiritual journey. This is my prayer to You. You have given me occult power. I wish to use it for their salvation. I don't want them to wallow in the pleasures of ignorance. These are my brothers and sisters. They are crying for light and illumination and I wish, with Your kind permission, to use my power to expedite their life's inner journey."

Now, when these three occultists left their bodies and passed behind the curtain of Eternity, God said to the first one, "I don't need you. I don't want you. The world of greed needs you. Go away. You are meant for the world of greed and temptation."

To the second occultist, God said, "I don't want you. I don't need you. The world of curiosity needs you. You are a miracle-monger. Go to the world of miracles. I don't need you."

To the third one, who had helped the sincere seekers in their spiritual pursuit, God said, "I need you. I need you badly. You have served Me. You have served the divinity in humanity. I need you. You are Mine."

Occultism deals with power. Unfortunately, in the West, occultism has been a victim of misunderstanding. Here in the West you have seen that black magic has taken the place of occultism. Proper occultism will never destroy anyone; nor will it create any calamity for anybody. But black magic, which is the lowest form of occultism, has created millions and millions of problems. I personally knew six or seven persons who were victims of black magic. In merciless ways they were attacked by some black magicians. They came to me for help. I did help them and they are now free. Now, many people will be under the impression that all this was done by real occult power. Real occult power would not create this kind of problem. It is black magic in the lowest vital plane that creates all these problems.

So, when an occultist lives in the soul and works for the soul, he is a divine occultist. But when an occultist lives in the vital and works for the fulfillment of the vital—lower vital, emotional vital, impure vital—then he is not living for the soul. He is living to satisfy his own ego, which is undivine, unrefined, obscure, impure and evil.

A genuine seeker of truth and light will not cry for occult power. Everybody has to realize God; but if someone says that occult power is necessary in order to realize God, he is committing a deplorable mistake. There are many occultists who have not realized God. Yes, in the far distant future, everybody has to realize God. No son of God, no human being, will remain unrealized.

What is of paramount importance is God-Realization. After one realizes God, if God wants to give him occult power, he will not be able to misuse it. A sincere seeker will cry only for God's Light, God-Realization and God-Fulfillment. He will never cry for occult power.

You all know of the great spiritual Master, Sri Ramakrishna. His dearest disciple was Swami Vivekananda. Once the great Master said to his dearest disciple, "Naren, I have all kinds of occult powers. I want to give you some of my occult powers."

Immediately the disciple said to his Master, "Please tell me, will these occult powers help me in my God-Realization?"

The Master said, "Oh, no. Occult power has nothing to do with God-Realization, but if you want to do some work here on earth, at that time occult power can be of some use."

Then Vivekananda said, "No, I want to realize God first—first things first."

So in the spiritual life, a real spiritual seeker will not cry for this kind of occult power. He will cry only for God-Realization. And if God wants that particular person to work for Him, naturally God will give him spiritual power, inner power, to manifest Him on earth.

If one really wants God, if one really wants the transcendental Truth, then one must enter into the realm of Yoga. Yoga means union with God. Once we become consciously inseparable from our divine, unlimited consciousness, then we can see, feel and grow into our highest Reality. And the manifestation of this Reality is our birthright.

There are two things we always observe: the power of love and the love of power. When we enter into the lowest form of occultism, we see the love of power. We do not have to go very far to see the love of power in politics; and in our daily activities also we are exercising our love of power. But the power of love is something different. In the power of love, it is love that exercises power sweetly, divinely and unconditionally. That is the power of love.

Now, a spiritual man, a sincere seeker after the truth, will care only for the power of love and not for the love of power. When he is one with God, with the Infinite Consciousness, he will see the power of love. But those who want to show the world their capacity, those who want to exercise their power of ego, will naturally cry for the love of power.

We know that when the power of love divinely replaces the love of power, man will have a new name: God.

ULTIMATELY EVERYTHING
BECOMES BORING

Ultimately everything
  Becomes boring.
Even great miracles
  Become boring.
Even the tremendous powers of the cosmic gods
  Become boring.
Even God the Omniscient
  Becomes boring.
Even God the Omnipotent
  Becomes boring.
  But, but, but
God the All-Love
  Never becomes boring.
      Never.

MIRACLE

What? Do I have to see any miracle?
Am I not the world's greatest miracle?
Who can equal me in performing miracles?
One miracle I have already shown:
I was the God supreme,
And now I am a feeble man.
My second miracle will take place
In the distant future:
I shall become
Once more the Lord of the Universe.

THE INNER PROMISE

University of Essex, Colchester, England
November 17, 1970

The inner promise is a seeker's inner progress. This progress inspires him, energizes him and helps him to please God in God's own way. The outer promise we make quite often, but the inner promise we make no more than once or twice during our life span. The outer promise we make, but the inner promise we keep. We try to live up to this inner promise and we try to manifest it on earth.

The outer promise we make to ignorance, to teeming ignorance; but the inner promise we make to God.

Our outer promise is to torture the world either consciously or unconsciously, or to try to destroy the world.

To change the face of the world and to fulfill the world with the Divine Will: this is the inner promise that we have made to God.

Now, there are three significant steps to this inner promise:

God is to be seen.
God is to be felt.
God is to be realized.

To see God, we have to be far, far away from the snares of darkness and ignorance.

To feel God, we have to live in the domain and realm of aspiration, the mounting flame within us.

To realize God, we have to grow into divine, constant and supreme surrender.

After we have attained God-Realization, there are two most significant steps, two more significant promises, we have to make. These promises are God-Revelation and God-Manifestation.

God-Revelation is the promise made by God-Realized souls on the strength of their unconditional concern for suffering humanity.

God-Manifestation is the unconditional promise of God-Realized souls to love mankind unconditionally and to manifest the Reality of Divinity here on earth.

In our day-to-day life, we see a child making promises to his mother: he won't tell a lie, he won't do anything wrong. But unfortunately he does tell lies, he does make mistakes. Yet the mother has boundless patience. She feels that sooner or later her child will tell the truth and do everything right. Then, as a young boy, a teen-ager, he does quite a few things wrong and he promises his parents that he will not do them anymore. Unfortunately, he again fails to keep his promise. But his parents still have the capacity to forgive him. They feel that either today or tomorrow he will turn over a new leaf. This is the inner confidence that they have in their son.

In the spiritual life also, many seekers make an inner promise, an inner commitment. They say they will enter into the spiritual life and give real importance to the life of purity, the life of aspiration, the life of realization. But, unfortunately, they fail to fulfill their promise. Nevertheless, God's boundless Compassion never abandons them. God, with His adamantine Will and Vision of the ever-transcending Beyond, sees that these seekers will sooner or later enter onto the right path and walk, march, run toward the Destined Goal.

Then there are some advanced seekers who have made considerable progress in their inner life, and who have made a promise to their own inner beings and to God that they will not give up their spiritual quest until they have realized God. God-Realization is their sole aim. But as ill-luck would have it, after having some higher experiences, they do not want to march further. They feel that these experiences are more than enough, at least for this life. So they do not want to go any further. They do not need or do not want God-Realization at this point, so God-Realization remains a far cry for them.

But God knows that these seekers entered into the spiritual life with utmost sincerity and made considerable progress. Only now they do not want to run toward their Destined Goal. They do not want to reach the farthest end of the Golden Shore.

Again God, with His boundless Compassion, observes the situation and tells the seekers, "Look, you will never be fulfilled. You will never see the face of satisfaction until you have seen the Golden Shore. You have not fulfilled your promise. But My Promise to you is unconditional. I shall wait for you. I shall take you, carry you to the destined shore of the Golden All at My choice Hour. If you do not want to run fast, faster, fastest, it is up to you; but you have to know that nobody on earth can remain unrealized, unfulfilled."

Each individual has to realize the highest Truth, but he who aspires will naturally reach the Goal sooner than the others who are still in the world of sleep.

Most of us are extremely clever as human beings, but not wise. We try to deceive other human beings. Not only that, we go to the length of deceiving our Inner Pilot, God. In spite of knowing that we can never, never deceive the Inner Pilot, we unconsciously and sometimes even consciously try to deceive the Inner Pilot, God. We tell God, "O God, if You give us some inner wealth [that is to say, Peace, Light and Bliss], we shall offer half of it to mankind. We shall not use it all for ourselves." It is just like saying to God, "If You give me a dollar, I will give half to mankind and keep only half for myself."

Now, God observes our sincerity. He examines the face of our sincerity and sees whether we are really sincere. And what happens? God gives us some Peace, Light, Bliss and other divine qualities, but we feel that it is not satisfactory. What do we do? Immediately we say, "O God, You have not given me the full amount, the full quantity. I wanted to have a dollar, but You have given me only half a dollar. You are very clever. You have already kept half a dollar for Yourself, that is to say, for humanity. So I don't have to give humanity the Peace, Light and Bliss that I already have."

How we try to deceive the divinity in humanity! Everybody here at this place has something to offer: Peace, Light, Bliss, sincerity, simplicity. There is nobody on earth who is not in a position to help the rest of mankind. This help, this service, if I can use the term "service," can be offered by any individual here on earth.

If somebody feels that he is more sincere than somebody else, then let his sincerity be shared with other persons.

If somebody feels that he is purer than somebody else, than his neighbors or friends, then let him share his purity.

If somebody feels that he has more aspiration than his friends or neighbors, then let him share it.

That is the promise that we can make to God at every moment.

Then we come to realize that every time the soul enters into the field of creation and manifestation, it makes a most solemn promise to God, the Pilot Supreme, to try its utmost to reveal God here on earth. But, unfortunately, when the soul enters into the world, the sea of ignorance tries to envelop the soul. Then the body, vital, mind and heart consciously or unconsciously get pleasure in identifying themselves with the ignorance-sea. But the soul is all-forgiving. It does not cast aside the body, vital, mind and heart. It has boundless patience.

If this body, vital, mind and heart identify themselves with the soul, and if they want to see the Truth with the soul's eye—if that is their promise, their only promise, their inner promise—then the date of God-Realization, God-Revelation and God-Manifestation on earth is not very far off.

Each individual can make a solemn promise to himself and to humanity at large. This is a promise of dedicated self-service. And when he fulfills his inner promise, God fulfills His highest Promise of absolute Perfection in and through the aspirant.

PROMISE

You are proud
That you are God's first promise.
He is proud
That he is God's last promise.
I am proud
That I am God's concealed promise.
God is proud
That He is far above His Promise.

YOUR PROMISE

Your promise to God
   Is God's highest Pride.
Your promise to man
   Is man's strongest anxiety.
Your promise to heaven
   Is heaven's nectar-delight.
Your promise to earth
   Is Earth's frustration-night.

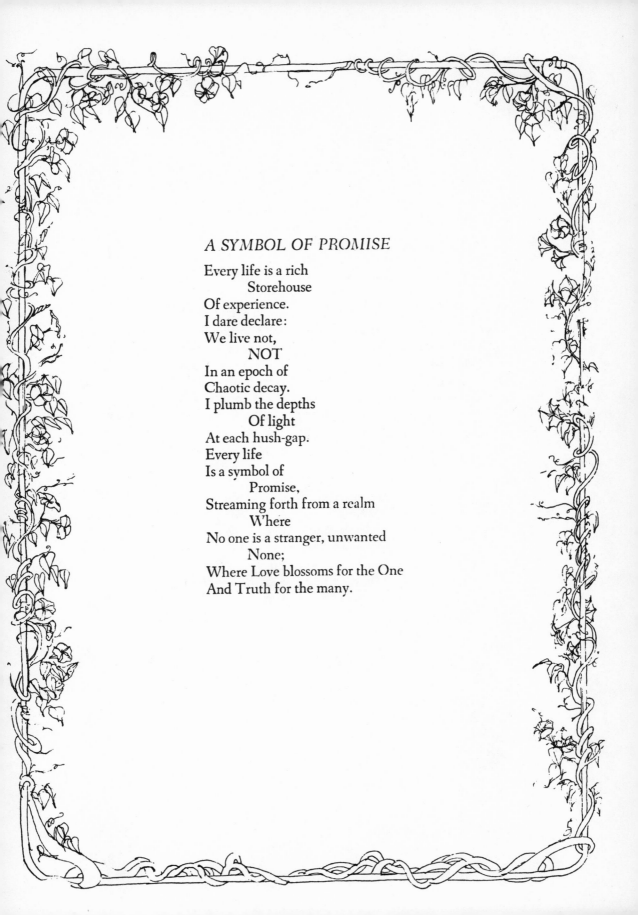

A SYMBOL OF PROMISE

Every life is a rich
      Storehouse
Of experience.
I dare declare:
We live not,
      NOT
In an epoch of
Chaotic decay.
I plumb the depths
      Of light
At each hush-gap.
Every life
Is a symbol of
      Promise,
Streaming forth from a realm
      Where
No one is a stranger, unwanted
      None;
Where Love blossoms for the One
And Truth for the many.

THE INNER TEACHING

University of Leeds, Leeds, England
November 18, 1970

We get the inner teaching either from a spiritual Master or from our own soul. It is infinitely easier for us to get this inner teaching from a spiritual Master, for we can speak to him and see him daily. He understands our language. He is one with us. Although in the inner world he is infinitely superior to us, he is in us and for us. His inner consciousness is flooded with Peace, Light and Bliss. But we have to know that a day shall dawn when the message of the soul and the spiritual Master's teaching must go together. There can be no difference, not an iota of difference, between their teachings.

But unless and until one has the capacity to dive deep within, it is always better and safer to listen to one's Master. It is not that one has to have a spiritual Master all his life. No. For just a while, especially at the beginning, one must have a spiritual Master. When the seeker himself realizes the highest Truth, he does not need any spiritual guidance. He himself grows into effulgent light. The inner soul within him comes to the fore and leads him, guides him and molds him, perfecting his inner and outer nature.

The inner teaching. The inner teaching teaches us how to love mankind and how to serve the divinity in humanity.

Simplicity, sincerity and purity. These are the three things that we need in our inner life. Simplicity, sincerity and purity.

Simplicity we need at every moment. For if the mind is not simple, if the mind is complicated and complex, then there can be no peace in the mind. A child is simple. He is all joy. In our day-to-day existence, unfortunately, we do not pay any attention to simplicity. If we go deep within, if we have a simple mind, a simple existence, we shall feel how lucky, how happy and fortunate we are.

Sincerity is the life of our heart. If we have sincerity, then we have to know that we are already marching toward our Destined Goal. Sincerity is our safeguard. A sincere seeker is running toward his Destined Goal, either consciously or unconsciously, at every moment. If we want to make constant progress here on earth, then what we need is a sincere heart.

Purity. Purity in the body. This purity does not mean that we have to take a bath ten times a day. No. It is the inner purity that we need and not just the outer cleanliness. When we are pure, we can receive the divine Peace, Light, Bliss and Power in abundant measure. When we can maintain our purity, then Peace, Joy, Light, Bliss and Power can dawn on earth. The whole role of purity is of paramount importance in our spiritual life.

In the inner life we see the role of fear and doubt, courage and certainty.

Fear. What is it? When we follow the spiritual life, we come to realize sooner than at once that fear is a real enemy. What does it do? It buys our coffin long before we are destined to die.

Doubt. What does it do? It starts digging our grave while we are still alive, while we are still performing our earthly duties.

Courage. Courage is our inner indomitable will. The outer expression of our inner indomitable will is manifested in the form of outer courage. Each moment we can see the reality, stand in front of the reality and grow into the reality if our existence is inundated with the inner will and the outer courage.

Certainty. God is ours. God is not the sole monopoly of an individual. It is not that only realized souls can dare to claim that God belongs to them. No, far from it. Each individual has the right to proclaim that God is his and that he belongs to God. He has to feel that God and he are eternally one and that God-Realization is his birthright.

The inner teaching. What do we learn from the inner teaching? Aspiration. Aspiration is the inner flame, the mounting cry within us. Each individual has this burning flame within. But unfortunately most of us do not take the trouble to use the flame of aspiration within us. We are fond of using something else in our day-to-day life: desire.

Desire is something that binds us.

Aspiration is something that frees us.

The message of desire is to possess and be possessed.

The message of aspiration is to expand, enlarge and immortalize our earthly existence.

When we desire, we live in the world of anxieties, worries, frustrations, limitations, bondage and death. When we aspire, we live in our divine consciousness here on earth. We feel the message and life-breath of Infinity, Eternity and Immortality. These are not vague terms; far from it. He who prays, he who meditates, he who concentrates, he who contemplates daily can easily enter into the domain of Infinity, Eternity and Immortality. His consciousness is bound to be flooded with Infinity's Peace, Eternity's Light and Immortality's Bliss.

The outer knowledge tells us how we can lord it over the world, how we can destroy the world. But the inner knowledge tells us how we can be inseparably one with God's entire Creation. The inner teaching means inseparable oneness, not only with the Creator, but also with His Creation.

The inner teaching is very simple. As my introducer was kind and wise enough to say, real Indian philosophy is not complicated, but people make it complicated and then they misunderstand it. The inner teaching has also at times been expressed in complicated terms, but it is very, very simple. Anyone can learn the inner life, can try to live the inner life. Anyone can fulfill his inner existence, his divine existence here on earth.

Philosophy is not the answer to the inner life. Nor is religion the answer. Philosophy helps. Religion too helps to some extent. But spirituality—let us use the term Yoga, a Sanskrit word—is by far the best answer to the inner life. Yoga means union, conscious union, with God. If we cry for conscious union with God, then without the least possible hesitation we can easily live the inner life.

Philosophy: let us use the Sanskrit word *darshan,* which means to envision or see. One of India's greatest spiritual Masters, Sri Ramakrishna, said, "In days of yore people used to have visions. Now people study *darshan!*" This is the difference between the Vedic seers, who had the highest illumined vision, and those who just study philosophy.

Religion: When we go deep inside religion, without fail we get the message of truth; but we do not do it. I say, "My Hinduism is by far the best." Immediately you tell me, "Stop! Stop! No comparison. Christianity is by far the best." Then a follower of Judaism will contradict us both. He will say, "No, Judaism is by far the best." So this goes on, with no end. This is our outer teaching. Each one is right in his own limited way.

But we have to have the inner oneness, the inseparable oneness with God and His Creation. We can consciously achieve this oneness only through real prayers, concentration, meditation and contemplation. Yoga transcends all religions. Religion is right in its own way. Philosophy is right in its own way. Philosophy can lead us right up to the door. Religion can lead us a few steps inside the room. But real meditation and spirituality, Yoga, not only leads us right up to the throne, but makes us sit on the throne itself.

When you follow the path of Yoga, you will see that there is no quarrel, no conflict. I must add, however, that one has to follow the path meant for him, or conflicts will indeed arise. Each path claims to be by far the best. But a sincere seeker, if he is really a sincere seeker, will not find fault with any path.

As you know, there are three principal paths: Karma Yoga, the path of action and dedication; Bhakti Yoga, the path of love and devotion; and Jnana Yoga, the path of knowledge and wisdom. Again, in Jnana Yoga there is a special branch we call Raja Yoga, which you in the West call "mysticism."

But I wish to say that if we are true, sincere seekers, genuine seekers, and if we follow the path of love and devotion, we cannot say a single word against the seeker who is following the path of knowledge, because we know that all roads ultimately lead to Rome. I take one road and you may take some other road, but Rome is the Goal for both of us. Each road can lead the aspirant to his Destined Goal. So how can I contradict other paths? It is sheer foolishness on our part to scorn another's discovery.

Our inner teaching tells us that it is true that all paths will lead to Rome, to our Destined Goal, God. But there is a path that leads us faster than the other paths, and that is the path of love, devotion and surrender. All roads will lead us to our destination, but one can say that there are shortcuts. The path of love leads us much faster to our destination.

When we follow the path of love, we find our spiritual life, our inner life, most satisfactory. Here God is dearest to us, not because He is Omnipotent, Omnipresent or Omniscient, but because He is all Love. A child feels that his father is dearest to him precisely because he feels all love is inside his father. He does not care how great his father is, whether his father is the magistrate or barrister or president. Just because his father is all love to him, his father is dearest to him.

Similarly God, our Eternal Father, can be approached most successfully and in a way that seems most convincing, through love. When we approach Him through love, we see that He is all Love; and when we just open our eyes and try to look at Him, we see that He is right in front of us, blessing us, embracing us. He says, "My child, I have been all the time waiting for you." Here love means one's constant feeling of inseparable oneness with one's Beloved.

The end of all inner teaching is love: Divine Love, not human love. Human love binds; the result is frustration. And at the end of frustration, destruction looms large. But Divine Love is expansion, enlargement, the feeling of true oneness. So if we love someone, we have to know that we love him precisely because deep inside that person is God. It is not because the person is my father, or my mother, or my brother, or my sister. No. I love him just because inside him I feel, I see, the living presence of my dearest Beloved.

For those who want to follow the spiritual path, for those who want to feel God as their very own, I wish to say that Love Divine is the answer. In Love Divine the seeker's real fulfillment and perfect Perfection loom large and important. This is the easiest path. This love is most convincing, most effective. We all can practice the inner teaching by offering our true love to God, to the divinity inside humanity. The more we offer this Divine Love, the more we fulfill the Inner Pilot within and without us.

Life Divine is not a far cry here on earth. The fulfillment of Divinity here on earth can never remain a far cry if we know the secret of secrets. And that secret is to grow into the Divine Love, where the lover and the Beloved become one, the creation and the Creator become one, the finite and the Infinite become one.

It is here on earth that we shall hear the message of the soul-stirring flute of Infinity. We do not have to go to heaven; we do not have to go to any other realm of consciousness. Right here, here and now, we can hear the message of Liberation, Enlightenment and Divine Fulfillment if we follow the inner teaching, which is Love Divine: Love for Love's sake, Love for God's sake.

WHY DO I TEACH HIM?

Why do I teach him?
I teach him
   Because
I want him to see God
    Soon.
Why do I teach him?
I teach him
   Because
I want him to claim God
    Soon.
Why do I teach him?
I teach him
   Because
God is sleeplessly for him.

HE HAS HEARD HIS MASTER'S FOOTFALLS

His life is full of din,
His life is full of rush,
His life is full of hurry.
He is a picture of insincerity,
He is a picture of ingratitude,
He is a picture of failure.
He fails to silence the storm of his flesh,
He fails to come out of the abyss of his doubt,
He fails to bury the coffin of his fear.
     Yet
He shall be saved,
He shall be liberated,
He shall be fulfilled.
     For
He has heard his Master's footfalls.

MASTER

O Lord of Nature, sovereign Sun of all!
    Who, if not Thou, will speak of Thee?
    Thy smile of Grace through eternity
Frees all aspiring souls from night's dumb call.
Reality Unique! Thou art the ring
    Of the lowest chasm and spanless height.
    In Thee they feel their haven bright;
In Thee all beings move and wave and wing.
To see Thy all-transcending mystic Form
    No vision have we of golden gaze;
    Thou art the Noon of all our days,
The veerless Pilot in our death's stark storm.

A STUDENT FROM GOD'S SCHOOL

He studied at God's school;
God was his main teacher.
God taught him
Only one thing: necessity.
"Son, if you want to live
Only in the soul's world,
      Then
I am your only necessity.
But if you want to live
In the body's world,
Then everything is your necessity,
Everybody is your necessity,
I am your necessity,
Countless, yet countless more.
So, son, make your own choice.
Now that you have completed your studies,
The time has come for you to go home
And begin your life."

THE UNIVERSE

Keble College, Oxford, England
November 19, 1970

Oxford, to you I bow because you hold your tradition dear.
Oxford, to you I bow because you own English glory.
Oxford, to you I bow because you are the English pride.

Aum. Aum is God. *Aum* is the Inner Pilot. *Aum* is the universe.

Aum. Purnam adah, purnam idam, purnat purnam udacyate.
Purnasya purnam adaya purnam evavasisyate. The universe. "Infinity
is that. Infinity is this. From Infinity, Infinity has come into existence.
From Infinity, when Infinity is taken away, Infinity remains."

Marcus Aurelius said, "The man who does not know what the
universe is, does not know where he lives."

The universe.
The universe is God's Creation and man's realization.
The universe is God's Compassion and man's emancipation.
The universe is God's Concentration and man's transformation.
The universe is God's Meditation and man's revelation.
The universe is God's Contemplation and man's manifestation.

The poet in me tells me that the universe is beautiful.
The singer in me tells me that the universe is enchanting.
The philosopher in me tells me that the universe is meaningful.
The Yogi in me tells me that the universe is soulful.
The God-lover in me tells me that the universe is fruitful.

My poet sees the truth.
My singer feels the truth.
My philosopher achieves the truth.
My Yogi realizes the truth.
My God-lover becomes the truth.

Man's dictionary houses millions of words. But God's Dictionary has only two words: aspiration and receptivity. God out of His boundless Bounty offers these two most significant words—should I say this significant wealth—to mankind: aspiration and receptivity.

The aspiration of today is tomorrow's salvation.
The receptivity of today is tomorrow's infinity.

In the finite we have to hear the message of the Infinite.
In the fleeting second we have to hear the message of the eternal Beyond.
In the domain of death we have to hear the message of Immortality.

Here at this point the immortal poet Blake sings through us and for us:

> To see a world in a grain of sand
> And heaven in a wild flower,
> Hold infinity in the palm of your hand
> And eternity in an hour.

This is a message the spiritual seeker can cherish. His inner being and inner life can be surcharged with this message, which can reverberate in the inmost recesses of his aspiring heart.

The outer universe, the inner universe and the inmost universe. My physics friend, my chemistry friend, my geography friend, my astronomy friend all inform me about the outer universe. I am most grateful to them. My psychology friend and my philosophy friend tell me about the inner universe. I am most grateful to them. My Yogi friend and my Avatar friend tell me about the inmost universe. I am most grateful to them. I ask them all if they are totally satisfied with their achievements, discoveries and realizations. They flatly say, "No."

My friends in the outer universe tell me they have much more to discover and unravel. My friends in the inner universe tell me they have much more to embody and realize. And my friends in the inmost universe tell me they have much more to reveal and manifest.

The visible universe and the invisible universe. The thinker in us sees the visible universe with the aspiring mind. The knower in us feels the visible universe with the aspiring heart.

In order to enter into the invisible universe, what we need is the soul's illumining light. If we do not see with the soul's illumining light, if we do not listen to the dictates of our soul, it is simply impossible for us to enter the invisible universe.

The living universe and the evolving universe, the dying universe and the perishing universe. When we aspire, when we consciously, soulfully and spontaneously try to go beyond the boundaries of the finite, we live in the living and evolving universe. When we consciously or unconsciously cherish doubt, jealousy, fear, imperfections, bondage, limitations and death, we live in the dying and perishing universe.

If we want to live in the universe—the spiritual universe or the real universe—we have to know that we must abide by the laws of the universe.

What are the laws of the universe? Love and serve.

Love humanity. Serve divinity.

We have to love the humanity in divinity. We have to serve the divinity in humanity.

At this point we can recollect the message of Plato, who said, "Through obedience we learn to command." Now, if we obey the laws of the universe, then we can command ignorance and govern death.

The scientist wants to discover the entire universe. The spiritual person, the seeker of the infinite Truth, also wants to discover the entire universe. So the spiritual scientist and the spiritual seeker will always run together, for they have the same message.

The scientist of scientists, Einstein, offers us the most sublime message: "His life is worthwhile who lives for others." This is precisely what a spiritual person, a seeker of boundless Light and Peace, tells us. Only he who lives for others has a meaningful life. Verily this is the message of all hallowed religions: live for others.

Although science and religion run abreast in this respect, there is something else. We call it Yoga. *Yoga* is a Sanskrit word which means union: union with God, union with Infinity, Eternity and Immortality. When we enter into the field of Yoga we feel that the love and service we offer to mankind is not for others, but for us, for our enlarged part. There is no such thing as "others." All are members of the same family.

When we remain in the mire of ignorance, we say "I," "you," "him"; but when it is a matter of oneness—inseparable oneness, oneness with God, oneness with mankind, oneness with God's Creation—then we cannot say that it is for others. It is for our sake, for the sake of our enlarged and more complete self.

Discovery. Science will discover the truth. Religion—or should I say spirituality—will discover the truth in the universe. And Yoga, oneness with God, will realize the ultimate Truth for the universe.

When the discovery of science is complete, it will see that its universe is manifesting the Truth of the ultimate Beyond.

When religion or spirituality discovers the ultimate Truth, it will see that its universe is realizing the Truth of the ever-transcending Beyond.

And when Yoga, or conscious union with God and mankind, completes its journey, it will transform the face of the world. It will illumine the face of the earth.

The discovery of the scientist, the discovery of religion and spirituality, and the discovery of one's highest oneness, inseparable oneness with God, will run together like three brothers, speeding toward the eternal Father, the Goal.

APOCALYPSE

Within, without the cosmos wide am I;
In joyful sweep I loose forth and draw back all.
A birthless deathless Spirit that moves and is still
Ever abides within to hear my call.

I who create on earth my joys and doles
To fulfill my matchless quest in all my play,
I veil my face of truth with golden hues
And see the serpent night and python day.

A consciousness bliss I feel in each breath,
I am the self-amorous child of the Sun.
At will I break and build my symbol sheath
And freely enjoy the world's unshadowed fun.

CURIOSITY OR NECESSITY

St. David's College, Lampeter, Wales
November 20, 1970

I am extremely happy, fortunate and proud to be here this evening in your midst. I shall be in the British Isles for about a month. If I had gone back to New York, where I live, without paying my respectful homage to Wales, it would have been the summit of my folly and ignorance.

I understand this is a small university—small in size, but not in height and depth. I understand that there are three hundred and fifty students here. I have been to Yale, Princeton, Cornell, Harvard and most of the other important universities in the States. There you will find thousands and thousands of students. But what we need is quality and not quantity. What we need is aspiration, the search for the Truth, and nothing else. When we have that inner cry for Truth, we do not need anything else.

Yesterday I was at Oxford. Today I am here. On the twenty-third I will be in Cambridge. Then I will be visiting Scotland, Ireland, France and Switzerland. What am I doing? I am doing only one thing. Like a bird I am flying from one place to another. My wings are love and service. One wing is love, the other wing is service. I try to love mankind. I try to serve mankind. This is what I have been doing so far. So I have come here to offer my love to the God inside you and to serve the divinity within you.

Curiosity or necessity. Curiosity is not necessity. Necessity is not curiosity. These two are like the North Pole and the South Pole. It is quite simple. A curious man does not want the truth. He does not need the truth. He just wants to hear from others what the truth looks like. On very rare occasions, he may want to see the truth from a distance. But he is afraid of personally approaching the truth. He feels that the moment he approaches the truth, the volcanic power of the truth will destroy him, his earthly existence. His earthly existence is nothing other than ignorance.

Curiosity commits two unpardonable sins. It kills our spontaneous love for light, the illumining light that transforms our life and enables us to realize the highest Truth. It also extinguishes our inner flame, which is a normal and natural fire. This inner flame we call aspiration. The higher this flame of aspiration rises, the sooner we reach the shores of the Golden Beyond.

Curiosity is afraid of two things: the highest reality and divinity. When reality—that is to say, the transcendental Reality—looks at curiosity, curiosity immediately runs away, looking for an escape, a hiding place. For curiosity feels that in no time it will be exposed. When divinity looks at curiosity, curiosity, out of tremendous fear, curses divinity. It feels that a perfect stranger is entering into its very breath.

Curiosity has, however, two intimate friends: doubt and jealousy. Doubt feeds curiosity just at the moment when the divine Peace, Love, Bliss and Power of the spiritual Master want to help mankind unconditionally. Doubt feeds curiosity at that very moment. Jealousy makes curiosity feel that it is far inferior to the genuine seekers of the infinite Light. So jealousy does not permit curiosity to make friends with the spiritual seekers or to take spiritual help from them. Jealousy

says, "If the spiritual seeker or Master is so great, then what of it? Let me remain in the meshes of ignorance. No harm." Here jealousy leads curiosity to remain where it already is.

Now let us focus our attention on necessity, divine necessity. Necessity is spirituality and spirituality is necessity.

What is spirituality? It is the common language of man and God. Here on earth we have hundreds and thousands of languages to allow one person to understand another; but when it is a matter of God and man, there is only one language, and that language is spirituality. If one follows the path of spirituality, one can easily speak to God face to face.

Necessity, divine necessity, is the pressure to see the highest and to feel the deepest. Today we see the highest, tomorrow we feel the deepest, and the day after we grow into the highest and into the deepest.

God is not only *a* necessity, but *the* necessity. How and why is God *the* necessity? We know that everything has failed us or will fail us in one way or another. But God has never failed the sincere seekers of the infinite Truth. So if we really cry for the inner Truth, the infinite Truth, God will not fail us.

From mankind we expect perfection, perfect Perfection. Now, no person on earth is absolutely perfect. Then how can we expect perfect Perfection from anyone? We expect absolute divinity from human beings, but absolute divinity is still a far cry for the individual. But if we want to see perfect Perfection, absolute divinity, only God can show it to us. He can show us His absolute Divinity. What is more, He can offer us His perfect Perfection, His absolute Divinity.

Today's desire compels us to deny and avoid the Truth, God. Tomorrow's aspiration will compel us to see God the Divinity, God the Inner Pilot. There can be no choice.

Now, what do we mean when we say God is the only reality, or God is the necessity, the only necessity? When we speak of God, what do we actually mean? We mean God-Realization or self-discovery. Let us use the term God-Realization. God-Realization is not only possible but practicable; and what is more, it is inevitable.

The outer cry we have. With our outer cry we feel that satisfaction is possessing and being possessed.

With our inner cry we enlarge ourselves, we expand ourselves, we fulfill God here on earth.

The immortal poet Shakespeare said,

> Teach thy necessity to reason thus;
> There is no virtue like necessity.

Necessity is the greatest blessing. We cannot fathom the depth of necessity.

> Man's necessity is God.
> God's necessity is man.

Man needs God for his highest transcendental realization, and he will have it in God. God needs man for His absolute Manifestation here on earth. We need God to realize our highest truth or highest existence. God needs us to manifest Him here on earth, totally, divinely and supremely.

Without realizing God we cannot have abundant Peace, Light, Bliss and Power. God-Realization is of absolute necessity here. Without God, we remain unrealized. Similarly, without man, God remains unmanifested.

Philip Sidney said, "Thy need is greater than mine." When we follow the spiritual life, when we walk along the path of spirituality, one word constantly looms large and important, and that word is *sacrifice*. We have to sacrifice our very existence for others—what we have and what we are. What we have is willingness and what we are is cheerfulness. This cheerfulness we can have only when we go deep within. When we are cheerfulness within, we are willingness without. If our inner existence is flooded with joy and delight, then only shall we be eager, more than eager to help the outer world. If there is a barren desert within us, if there is no light within us, how are we going to help or serve mankind? So, if we have joy within, sooner or later we can bring this joy to the fore and offer it to mankind. We have to love mankind soulfully, serve mankind unconditionally. God-Realization is of the utmost importance. First things first; and our first necessity is God-Realization or self-discovery.

As I said before, curiosity is not necessity, curiosity is not spirituality. But we cannot be sincere overnight. If I am not sincere, I cannot become sincere in the twinkling of an eye. If I have not realized the truth, I cannot realize the truth overnight. It is impossible. But if out of curiosity I want to see what is happening in the sincere spiritual seekers who feel that God is the only necessity, then I can try to act sincere myself, because I see something divine and fulfilling in them.

So if out of curiosity one goes to a sincere spiritual seeker or a spiritual Master, then he may see something which he has not seen before, in him or around him. I have some students or acquaintances who come to me with very limited aspiration; I beg to be excused. I must say that I also have most sincere students and disciples. But I do not throw cold water on those who are right now unfortunate and do not have genuine aspiration. I tell them, "Don't worry. If you have come to me just out of curiosity, no harm. Mix with the sincere seekers. See what they are getting from their genuine spiritual life; and if you feel that their spiritual life has changed their nature or is giving them a new light and peace, giving a new meaning to their outer life, then try to follow their example. Be one with them."

I have come across quite a few totally and exclusively curious human beings who have been transformed into serious, sincere seekers. Truth, either today or tomorrow, has to be realized; and if we do not have utmost sincerity right now, no harm. Sincerity grows. Everything grows. Like a muscle, everything can be developed. If we do not have implicit aspiration right now, no harm. We can develop aspiration, our inner cry.

So, dear sisters and brothers, here I am seeing many, many sincere seekers. To them I say: run fast, faster, fastest toward your Destined Goal. And, I beg to be excused, here I am seeing one or two, very few, curious seekers. To them I say: do not stop with the achievement which is your curiosity. Please try to go one step further. Then you will see today's curiosity transformed into tomorrow's sincerity, and in your sincerity you will see the inner cry, the mounting flame which we call aspiration.

Today's aspiration is tomorrow's realization. This is the only truth. This is the only realization that I can offer to you, dearest sisters and brothers, seekers of the Infinite Truth. Start here and now.

I NEED

I need.
I need my Mother's Love.
I need.
I need my Father's Wisdom.
I need.
I need my Master's Light.
I need.
I need my God's Compassion.
What else do I need?
Nothing, absolutely nothing!

THE HIGHER WORLDS

King's College, Cambridge, England
November 23, 1970

Cambridge, I bow to your aspiration-height. I bow to your knowledge-light. I bow to your divine pride. True, you are in England, you are of England, but you are also of the world at large. The entire world claims you as its very own.

There are seven higher worlds and seven lower worlds. The higher worlds are *Bhur, Bhuvar, Swar, Jana, Mahar, Tapas* and *Satya*. One of the Upanishads names seven higher regions. These are *Agniloka, Vayuloka, Varunaloka, Adityaloka, Indraloka, Prajapatiloka* and *Brahmaloka*. Certain spiritual figures are of the opinion that the first-mentioned group of worlds corresponds to the second. Others, equally qualified, dispute this. Strangely enough, all without exception agree that the world *Satya* and *Brahmaloka* are one and the same.

We can enter into these worlds on the strength of our aspiration and receptivity. When we have aspiration and receptivity, these worlds can never remain a far cry.

Aspiration. What do we mean by this term? The inner cry, the mounting flame within us. Aspiration is reality's constant necessity.

Receptivity. How can we have receptivity? We can have receptivity if we grow into purity and sincerity. When sincerity and purity loom large and important in our earthly existence, then we can easily have receptivity.

A sincere seeker needs aspiration and receptivity. Without aspiration, he is rootless. Without receptivity, he is fruitless.

The higher worlds. Each individual seeker has the divine right to enter into the higher worlds. His aspiration can easily guide him and lead him to God's Throne. To enter into the high, higher, highest worlds, what we need is the inner cry. We cry for name and fame. But if we inwardly cried for abundant Peace, Light and Bliss here on earth, then our entire being could be flooded with Peace, Light and Bliss.

These higher worlds are within us and not without. When we concentrate, when we meditate, when we contemplate, we enter into these higher worlds. When we concentrate dynamically, we near the door of these higher worlds. When we meditate soulfully, we enter into the Room Divine. When we contemplate unreservedly and unconditionally, we reach God's Throne.

Since we aspire to enter into the higher worlds, we pray to the cosmic gods. We feel that the cosmic gods will come to our aid and help us enter the higher worlds.

Here at this point I would like to invoke the soul of Marcus Aurelius: "Either the gods have the power to assist us or they have not. If they have not, what does praying to them signify? If they have, why do you not pray that they would remove your desires rather than satisfy them, set you above fear rather than keep away the thing you are afraid of?"

Now, if we want to enter the higher worlds in order to fulfill our desires, then we can never enter the higher worlds. We can enter the higher worlds only when it is the Will of our Inner Pilot, the Lord Supreme. When we go deep within, when we meditate for a couple of hours, if our meditation is most soulful and, at the same time, unconditional, then we will envision the higher worlds. No sincere seeker of the highest Truth, the ultimate Truth, will be denied the higher worlds.

Porphyry throws additional light on the matter: "We must ask of God only such gifts as are worthy of God, that is to say, such things as we cannot obtain from any except God."

In order to enter into the higher worlds, what we need is sincerity; what we need is purity; what we need is peace; what we need is delight.

Sincerity: Inner beauty's other name is sincerity.
Purity: The name of God's first child is purity.
Peace: Peace is unity's sovereignty and multiplicity's divinity.
Delight: Delight is the name of God's permanent Home.

There are two things we observe in our day-to-day life: the human and the divine. In everything we do, say or grow into, we see either the human or the divine.

The human world and the divine world. A clever man is he who knows how to deal with the outer world. He does not want to be deceived by the world, by mankind; but unconsciously or consciously he deceives the world, the world of ignorance. A wise man is he who knows all about the inner world, the higher worlds within. He does not deceive anybody. He wants to conquer the outer world, the world of ignorance. But his is not the conquest of Caesar: "I came, I saw, I conquered"—*Veni, vidi, vici.* Far from it. When a wise man wants to conquer ignorance, he does so only because his inner being compels him to transform the face of the world. He does not take pride in conquering the world. No. Feeling the breath of ignorance, he feels it is his bounden duty to transform ignorance into knowledge, darkness into light, death into immortality.

There are two ways to enter into the higher worlds. One is the way of knowledge, the other is the way of devotion.

Knowledge: I am the knowledge, I am the known, I am the knower.

Devotion: I am devotion, I am dedication, I am salvation.

Knowledge enlarges itself, expands itself into Infinity. Devotion identifies itself with the absolute Truth. On the strength of its identification, devotion grows into Infinity.

A sincere seeker of the ultimate Truth can follow either the path of knowledge or the path of devotion. But at the end of the journey's close, the seeker who follows the path of knowledge and the seeker who follows the path of devotion will meet and shake hands, because they have reached the selfsame Goal.

We live either in the world of human thought or in the world of Divine Will. Human thought slows down and dies out, but the Divine Will constantly grows and swiftly flows.

Similarly, human power is born of futility. Divine power is born of reality.

Finally we observe our love: human love and Divine Love. Human love is an express train: destination—frustration. Divine Love is a local train: destination—Illumination. Human physical love is slow poison. Divine Love is the running stream and the unceasing source of nectar. Human love can be transcended. Divine Love can be manifested. Human love is fruitless expectation. Divine Love is fulfilled perfection.

Unconditional love is what God is.
Unreserved devotion is what man needs.
Mutual surrender is what God and man offer one another.

When the power of love replaces the love of power, man will have a new name: God.

The Golden Hour, God's Hour, is dawning fast. Let us offer our heart's aspiration to the lofty realization of the seers of the hoary past,

Anandadd hy eva khalv imani bhutani jayante,
Anandena jatani jivanti,
Anandam prayantyabhisam visanti.
From Delight we came into existence.
In Delight we grow.
At the end of our journey's close, into Delight we shall retire.

My Rose Petals

LEAVE ME ALONE

Leave me alone, leave me alone.
I need my rest in my soaring nest.
My bleeding heart for God's bending ears.
His Heart my Host, His Soul my Guest.

Leave me alone, my play is done.
O world, no more shall I stab your pride.
Your lessons wild are harrows of death
I shall unlearn—in God to hide.

Leave me alone, leave me alone.
I have now seen my goal's highest Soul.
In the glow and flow of Silence-sea
My life of cries has found its role.

THE PILGRIMS OF THE LORD SUPREME

We are the Pilgrims of the Lord Supreme
On the Path of Infinity.
At this time we have broken asunder
Obstruction's door.
We have broken asunder the Night of
Tenebrous darkness, inconscience,
And the eternal, indomitable fear of death.
The Boat of the Supernal Light's Dawn is beckoning us,
And the World-Pilot of the hallowed bond
Of Love Divine is beckoning us.
The Liberator's Hands are drawing us to
The Ocean of the Great Unknown.
Having conquered the Life-Breath of
The Land of Immortality,
And carrying aloft the Banner of the Lord Supreme,
We shall return—we, the drops and flames
Of Transformation-Light.

HE

His actions
Interpret God.
His silence
Represents God.
He has reached
The Highest.
He stands beside
The Highest.
And you know
Where he started from.
He started from
The lowest,
The very
Lowest.

HOW TO CONQUER DOUBT

University of Dundee, Dundee, Scotland
November 25, 1970

A great writer once said, "A philosopher is one who doubts." In my humble opinion, we are all philosophers, for there is nobody on earth who has not doubted at least once.

The Sanskrit word for *philosophy* is *darshan*. *Darshan* means vision, to envison the truth. Sri Ramakrishna said, "In days of yore people used to have visions. Now people study *darshan!*" It is one thing to study the Truth; it is another thing to have the direct vision of the highest ultimate Truth.

Now, I am in no way throwing cold water on the students of philosophy—far from it. I also happen to be an insignificant philosopher. But what I wish to say is this: philosophy leads us to spirituality, and spirituality offers us God-Realization and self-discovery. So let us start our journey with philosophy. This is the first rung of the spiritual ladder. The next rung is spirituality, and the final rung is God-Realization.

Doubt. Doubt means absence of real knowledge. Real knowledge is true light, and true light is our inseparable oneness with the world.

Faith and doubt. These are like the North and the South Pole. Unfortunately, a man of faith is very often misunderstood. We are apt to call a man of faith a fanatic. Here we make a deplorable mistake. A fanatic hates reason and ignores the reasoning mind; whereas a man of faith, if he is really a man of faith, will welcome reason and accept the doubting mind. Then his faith will help the doubting mind to transcend itself into the infinite vast, into something eternal and immortal. This is what faith offers to the doubting mind.

A man of faith is also a man of divine humility. The farther he advances spiritually on the strength of his faith, the deeper he grows into the supreme humility.

Here at this point I wish to quote Keats' immortal utterance, "My greatest elevations of soul every time make me humble."

Doubt is our self-imposed ignorance. Faith is our inner vision of the ultimate Truth. Faith is our soul's expansion and soul's illumination.

We see darkness all around. We see impurity all around and imperfection all around. Again, it is we who have the inner inspiration, aspiration, capacity and adamantine will to transform the very face of the earth. How? By conquering doubt, our self-doubt; by conquering our doubt of humanity and of God.

Doubt. Why do we doubt? We doubt because we do not have conscious oneness with somebody else, with the rest of the world. If somebody doubts me, shall I doubt him in return? If I doubt him, then I sail in the same boat. But if I offer him my faith, my implicit faith, then either today or tomorrow, sooner or later, I can transform his nature.

What do we learn from a tree? When we vehemently shake a tree, what does the tree do? The tree immediately offers us its flowers, its fruits. Now similarly if others torture us with their teeming doubts, let us offer them our snow-white faith. Then our snow-white faith will transform their life of teeming, darkening and darkened clouds of doubt.

With our eyes wide open we see that the world is ugly. With our ears wide open we hear that the world is impure. But we also have the mind. Let us use our mind or compel the mind to see only the right thing, the pure thing, unlike the eyes. Let us use our mind or compel the mind to hear only the right thing, the divine thing. It is the mind, the developed mind, the conscious mind, the illumined mind, that has the capacity in abundant measure to transport us to the highest regions of consciousness.

We are all under the laws of Mother Earth. Mother Earth is under the laws of heaven. Heaven is under the express law of God. But our doubt, our cherished doubt, is under its own law. Its law is frustration, and in frustration destruction looms large.

Why do we doubt? Because we are wanting in proper understanding. There was a great spiritual saint named Kavir, who said, "Listen to me, brothers. He understands who loves."

If we love, then we understand; and if we understand the truth, then we have neither the opportunity nor the necessity to cherish even an iota of doubt in our day-to-day existence.

We doubt God at our own sweet will. We doubt God precisely because we think He is invisible. We doubt Him because we think

He is inaudible. We doubt God because we think He is incomprehensible.

But to see Him, what have we done? To hear Him, what have we done? To understand Him, what have we done?

To see Him, have we prayed soulfully every day? The answer is no. To hear Him, have we loved mankind devotedly? No. To understand Him, have we served the divinity in humanity? No. We have not prayed to God. We have not loved mankind. We have not served the divinity in humanity. Yet we want to see God face to face. It is impossible.

God can be seen on the strength of our inner cry, which we call aspiration, the mounting flame within us. Every moment this flame is rising toward the highest. If we know how to cry within, then this flame will mount, will climb high, higher, highest; and while it is climbing it will illumine the world around.

There is an Indian proverb which I am sure most of you have heard: "A strong man fears his enemy when the enemy is far off; but when the enemy is near, he is no longer afraid." I wish to add that when doubt attacks a spiritually strong man, he becomes stronger, infinitely stronger. He does this by bringing to the fore his own soul's light, which energizes him to fight against doubt and conquer it.

There is another way to conquer doubt: by feeling at this very moment that we are children, children of God; and again, by feeling that God is a Divine Child playing with us. We are human children and He is a Divine Child.

A child does not doubt. He has implicit faith in his parents. He has implicit faith in everyone he comes across. We can play the same role in our day-to-day life. Let us play with God, the Divine Child. There can be no shadow of doubt in our life when we speak, eat and move around if we feel we have a Divine Child within us, sporting with us. We are not alone. There is someone playing with us at every moment. If we know and feel this, then doubt can never eclipse our mind.

A lover of God, an adorer of God, feels that deep within him, in the inmost recesses of his heart, there is an island of ecstasy; and this island can never be submerged by the floods of doubt, for his love has already made him one with this divine certitude.

A seeker of the highest order said, "Some say, 'He [God] is too far.' Some say, 'No. He is living here.' But I have found Him. He is in the cradle of love."

When we love God, our problem is over. True, we all do not see God face to face. But we can imagine for a fleeting second that God with all His Love abides in our dear and near ones. Let us try to see

the face of our Beloved in our dear ones. Where there is love, true
love, there is all oneness. Where there is oneness, there can be no
doubt—no darkening, no threatening, no destructive doubt.

How to conquer doubt. In order to conquer doubt, we have to
constantly purify our nature. This purification has to take place in our
physical. The body has to be purified constantly. It is not by taking six
or seven baths a day that we can purify the body. Our body will be
purified only when we feel a living shrine within us. Then we have to
install the living deity of light and truth within us. Then in no time
the body will be purified. At that time we will not have any doubt in
our body, or in our physical mind.

The vital. The vital has to play the role of divine dynamism. It is
dynamic energy that we have to offer to the vital, and not aggressive
and destructive power, in order to conquer doubt in the vital.

The mind. Each moment the mind has to be flooded with clarity
and right thinking. Each moment the mind has to consciously house
divine thoughts, divine ideas, divine ideals. Then doubt will not be
able to breathe in the mind.

The heart. Each moment we have to make the heart soulful so that
we can easily conquer doubt in the heart. The heart has to offer the

message of sacrifice for others, for the rest of the world. While sacrificing his very life-breath, a sincere seeker feels that he is not sacrificing anything, but rather is just expanding his own inner consciousness and fulfilling himself here on earth.

Doubt can be conquered. It has to be conquered. How? The only answer is constant and soulful concentration on the mind, meditation on the heart and contemplation on the entire being.

FAITH AND PERSONAL EFFORT

Lord, can faith be increased
By personal effort?
   "Yes, faith can be increased
   By personal effort
      Provided
   One knows the real meaning
   Of personal effort."
What is personal effort?
   "Personal effort is nothing but
   Unseen and unrecognized Grace."
What is other Grace,
I mean normal Grace?
   "That Grace is called
   Universal shower."

FAITH AND DOUBT

O what is faith and what is doubt?
Faith is life-sun beyond the grave.
Doubt is the battle lost, within, without.
A doubter cries: Me none can save.

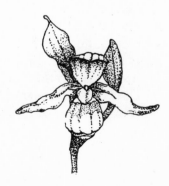

LOVE, DEVOTION AND SURRENDER

American International School, Zurich, Switzerland
November 27, 1970

Love is sweet, devotion is sweeter, surrender is sweetest.

Love is sweet. I have felt this truth in my mother's spontaneous love for me.

Devotion is sweeter. I have discovered this truth in my mother's pure devotion toward the perfection of my life.

Surrender is sweetest. I have realized this truth in my mother's constant surrender toward the fulfillment of my joy.

Again, love is mighty, devotion is mightier, surrender is mightiest.

Love is mighty. This truth I feel when I look at my father's face.

Devotion is mightier. This truth I discover when I sit at my father's feet.

Surrender is mightiest. This truth I realize when I live in the breath of my father's will.

Love, devotion and surrender. Saint Augustine has blessed us with a profound message: "Love and then do what you like."

Our mind thinks that this is absolutely true. Our heart feels that this is undeniably true. But unfortunately in our day-to-day life we are not able to practice it. That is to say, we do not know what love is. We do not know why we love something or someone. Finally, we do not know how to love.

What is love? From the spiritual and inner point of view, love is self-expansion. Human love binds and is bound. Divine Love expands and enlarges itself. Here we are dealing with Divine Love.

Devotion is the intensity in love, and surrender is the fulfillment of love. Why do we love? We love because at every moment we are pinched with hunger to realize the highest, to feel the inmost, to be consciously one with the universe, with the universal Truth, Light, Peace and Bliss, and to be completely fulfilled.

How to love? If we love with a view to achieving something from others, then our love is no love. Love means constant self-offering on the strength of our own inner aspiration.

This world of ours needs peace, joy, bliss, harmony and understanding. We feel that here on earth there is no light, no truth, no divinity—nothing of the sort. All the divine qualities, all aspects of the Lord Supreme, are in the skies, in the deep blue skies, not here: this is what we feel. Hence we always look up high for help. We feel that God is in heaven, not on earth. To rescue us, God will come down into the world. He is not to be found here on earth. Here we are wallowing in the pleasures of ignorance. There can be no light, no truth here.

But we must realize that, God being Omnipresent, He is here too. He is within us. He is also without. In the inmost recesses of our heart, we feel His living Presence.

As you all know, George Bernard Shaw has warned us, "Beware of the man whose God is in the skies." But our God is everywhere. He is not only in heaven, He is also here on earth. He is with us, He is within us and He is for us. We do not have to enter the highest regions of consciousness to see God. Our inner cry will bring to the fore our inner divinity, which is nothing other than God.

Surrender. Surrender is protection, and surrender is illumination. Surrender is our perfection. We begin our journey at the very commencement of our life. We surrender our existence to our parents and get, in return, protection. We listen to our parents. We surrender to their will, to their advice and suggestions, and we are protected, well protected. Joy boundless we feel in our day-to-day life when we are children. Why? Because we surrender our personal will, our own inner thinking, to our parents, and immediately we receive joy plus protection. In protection is joy, and in joy is protection.

Now, in the evening of our life what happens? If we follow the inner life and the spiritual life, in the evening of our life we also surrender. To whom? To the Inner Pilot, the Lord Supreme. At the end of our journey we surrender our very breath to the Supreme. Then we again get joy, perfect joy, unalloyed joy.

To quote Dante, "The happiest man is he who can connect the evening of his life with the beginning."

Now, if we are all sincere seekers of the ultimate Truth, then our journey begins with surrender to our parents, who are our well-wishers, our dearest and nearest ones. When we surrender our existence to them, we get joy in abundant measure. Then, when we walk along the path of spirituality, at every moment we try to listen to the dictates of our inner being. The more we listen to our inner being, the greater is our joy, and the higher our fulfillment. And then, when our term is over, when we have to enter into another world for a short rest, if we consciously surrender to God's Will, ours will be the supreme joy, the glory supreme.

It is difficult to love mankind. It is difficult to devote ourselves to mankind. It is difficult to surrender ourselves to mankind. This is true. In the same way, it is difficult to love God, to serve God, to devote ourselves to God and to surrender our living breath to God.

Now, why? The simple reason is that we want to possess and be possessed. We are constantly making ourselves victims of ignorance. That is to say, our desires can never be fulfilled. We have countless desires. God will fulfill only those desires that will be of some use, from which we will derive benefit. If He were to fulfill our countless desires, then He would be doing an injustice to our aspiring souls. That He will not do. He knows what is best for us and He has given us beyond our capacity, though unfortunately we are unaware of this.

Saint Francis, from his own experience, has offered a unique truth to the world at large: "He who thinks that God's Love is inadequate is very greedy." We are all really greedy people. If we go deep within, we see, we feel, we realize that God has given us infinitely more than we need and, needless to say, more than we deserve.

Love, devotion and surrender. These are the three rungs in the spiritual ladder, or should we say the ladder of our evolving consciousness. The first rung is love; the second, or penultimate, is devotion; and the ultimate is surrender.

A tiny drop enters into the ocean and becomes the mighty, the boundless ocean. Unfortunately, in the West surrender is misunderstood. We feel that if we surrender to someone, he will then lord it over us. We will have no individuality or personality. From the ordinary point of view, the human point of view, this is true. But from the spiritual point of view, it is absolutely wrong. When the finite enters into the Infinite, it becomes the Infinite all at once. When a tiny drop enters into the ocean, we cannot trace the drop. It becomes the mighty ocean.

Each moment we are given ample opportunity to love mankind. And if we really love mankind, then we have the feeling of wanting to offer devoted service to mankind. And when we really want to enlarge our existence, expand our consciousness and be one, inseparably one, with the Vast, then surrender is the only answer.

Each moment we see right in front of us a barrier between one human being and another—an adamantine wall between two people. We cannot communicate properly, wholeheartedly and soulfully. Why? Because we are wanting in love. Love is our inseparable oneness with the rest of the world, with God's entire Creation. We can break asunder this adamantine wall on the strength of our soulful love.

India's greatest poet, Rabindranath Tagore, said, "He who loves finds the door open." So our heart's door is already open for those who really, truly and soulfully love.

God loves us out of His Infinite Bounty, and His Heart's Door is always wide open. Just because He is all Love, we approach Him. He is our dearest, not because He is Omniscient and Omnipotent, but just because He is all Love.

Love, devotion and surrender.

To serve and never be tired is love.
To learn and never be filled is devotion.
To offer and never to end is surrender.

Love is man's reality.
Devotion is man's divinity.
Surrender is man's immortality.

Reality is all-pervading.
Divinity is all-elevating.
Immortality is all-fulfilling.

O, LOVE ME MORE AND LOVE ME LONG

O, love me more and love me long.
My boat is sinking; my hope is strong.
O, love me more and love me long.
My breath is bleeding; my dream is strong.
O, love me more and love me long.
My soul is leaving; my surrender strong.
O, love me more and love me long.
My Goal is crying; my promise strong.

ONE DAY

One day
Everybody will turn against him.
He knows it,
Yet he loves them.

One day
Everybody will hate him.
He knows it,
Yet he loves them.

One day
Everybody will leave him.
He knows it,
Yet he loves them.

One day
Everybody will try to end his life.
He knows it,
Yet he loves them.

One day
Everybody will destroy his breath.
He knows it,
Yet he loves them.

And after that
Everybody
Will love him dearly,
Adore him unreservedly
And
Claim him soulfully.
Alas, this is the common story
Of this uncommon world.

LOVE IS THIS, ALSO LOVE IS THAT

Love is the road that leads
Our souls to union vast.
Love is the passion-storm
That sports with our vital dust.
Love's child is emotion-flame.
Love's eyes are freedom, fear.
Love's heart is breath or death.
And love is cheap, love dear.

ANSWER ME

Answer me in one word:
    Who is God?
Answer me in two words:
    Where is God?
Answer me in three words:
    How to realize God?
Answer me in four words:
    How to become God?
        Who is God?
          Truth.
        Where is God?
          With Light.
        How to realize God?
          Through constant offering.
        How to become God?
          Through surrender-devotion-love.
The seeker's surrender
    Embodies God's Soul.
The seeker's devotion
    Embodies God's Heart.
The seeker's love
    Embodies God's Life.

THE MESSAGE OF SURRENDER

Today You have given me
The message of surrender.
I have offered to You
My very flower-heart.
In the dark night with tears,
In the unknown prison-cell of illusion,
In the house of the finite,
No longer shall I abide.
I know You are mine.
I have known this, Mother,
O Queen of the Eternal.

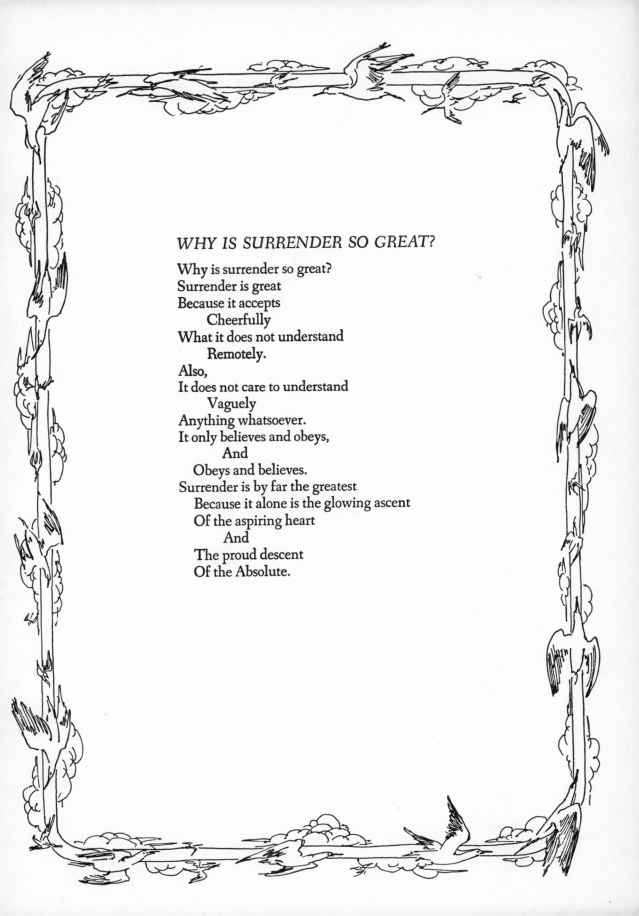

WHY IS SURRENDER SO GREAT?

Why is surrender so great?
Surrender is great
Because it accepts
    Cheerfully
What it does not understand
    Remotely.
Also,
It does not care to understand
    Vaguely
Anything whatsoever.
It only believes and obeys,
    And
  Obeys and believes.
Surrender is by far the greatest
  Because it alone is the glowing ascent
  Of the aspiring heart
    And
  The proud descent
  Of the Absolute.

FOUR MEMBERS IN MY FAMILY

I have four members
  In my family:
Fear and doubt,
Love and surrender.
Fear takes me
  From nothing-chasm
      To
    Nowhere-palace.
Doubt takes me
  From nowhere-sea
      To
    Nothing-shore.
Love takes me
  From fulfillment-land
      To
    Perfection-sky.
Surrender takes me
  From God-vision-seed
      To
    God-Reality-Tree.

THE PERMANENT
AND THE IMPERMANENT

University of Bristol, Bristol, England
November 20, 1970

What is permanent?
What is impermanent?
What is permanent is reality.
What is impermanent is non-reality.

Reality is the existence of light, in light and for light.
Non-reality is the existence of night, in night and for night.

Reality's parents are divinity and immortality.
Non-reality's parents are bondage and ignorance.

When we see the Divine Light, we feel happy. When we feel the Divine Light, we become strong. And when we grow into the Divine Light, our life becomes fruitful.

When we see the undivine night, we become weak, impotent. When we feel the undivine night, we feel sorry, we feel miserable. And when we grow into the undivine night, our life becomes meaningless, fruitless.

Illumining light and illumined light; darkening night and darkened night. Illumining light is the light that is within us. Illumined light is the light that is without us. Darkening night is the night that is before us. Darkened night is the night that is around us.

That which is real is permanent, and what is permanent is spiritual. What is spiritual? The life of the ever-transcending Beyond. But this life of the ever-transcending Beyond has to be manifested here on earth. This life is real; it is reality itself.

What is unspiritual? Let us use the term *material*. Something material is the wealth of the fleeting time.

Divine wealth and material wealth. Divine wealth is our inner aspiration. This aspiration is the song of Infinity, Eternity and Immortality within us. Material wealth is desire. It is the cry for immediate and constant possession. When we try to possess, unfortunately we feel that we are already possessed. But when we try to see someone with our soul's light, we feel that we are already liberated, and that he too is already liberated.

A thing permanent is divine. A thing impermanent is undivine. When divine wisdom dawns on earth, we will realize that an impermanent thing is useless.

Divinity and Immortality are within us. Immortality tells us what to do and Divinity tells us how to do it. Immortality tells us to listen to the dictates of our soul, which is a spark of the Supreme Light. It tells us to be always conscious of the Inner Pilot. Divinity tells us how we can do it. We can do it through a self-disciplined life, through dedication to a higher cause, through purification of our outer nature and through undying and unreserved love for God.

Bondage and ignorance are the parents of night. Ignorance tells us what to do and bondage tells us how to do it. Ignorance tells us to destroy the world, and bondage tells us how to do it—through cruelty and brutality and other unfair means.

A spiritual seeker tries to enter into the inmost recesses of his heart, and from there he tries to bring light to the fore. With the help of this light, he wants to grow into the breath of the permanent. Now, to grow into the breath of the permanent, what he needs is inner wisdom. What is this inner wisdom?

Lord Krishna, in the *Bhagavad-Gita*, the Song Celestial, says to Arjuna, his divine instrument, "O Arjuna, a wise man is he who has the mastery over the senses." That is to say, when we conquer our senses, we enter into the realm of wisdom, where reality grows and divinity flows.

To enter into the world of wisdom we need constant love: love for truth, love for light. But right now we are fond of fleeting truth, fleeting light, fleeting possessions. The fleeting wealth that we have or cherish is terribly afraid of truth. It doubts truth and it fears God. But our divine wealth, aspiration, invokes truth and adores God. Each day we are seeing with our own eyes and feeling with our own heart the impermanence of the man-made world. That is to say, the things that we create with our thoughts and the ideas that result from our actions do not last. This moment I have a thought and the next moment that thought is gone. Perhaps it gives me a result. This result lasts, again, for another fleeting second.

But there is something else which we call willpower: the soul's will, the adamantine will of the soul. If we can exercise an iota of this willpower, then we will see that not only the action but also the result is an everlasting reality. In order to develop the willpower of the soul, we have to enter into the life of the Spirit. We have to have a self-disciplined life. A self-disciplined life does not mean the mortification of life or a conscious torture of life. A self-disciplined life means a life that needs the Light and wants to be guided, molded and shaped by the Light. When the life is disciplined, we shall not act like animals. When the life is disciplined enough, the real divinity will grow. At that time we can say that God-Realization or self-discovery is our birthright, and in God-Realization we acquire the wisdom of the everlasting Truth.

It is not that one individual or some individuals are chosen to realize the highest Truth. No, far from it. Each individual is an instrument of God; but he has to be conscious. Right now he is not; he is unconscious. But when he prays, when he meditates, he automatically becomes a constant, conscious instrument of God. And he who becomes a conscious instrument of God hears in the very heart of the finite the message of the Infinite, and feels in the fleeting the Breath of the Eternal.

To think of God, to meditate on God constantly, is to live in God unreservedly. When we live in God constantly, soulfully and unreservedly, God unconditionally does everything for us. In infinite measure He offers His Light, Peace and Bliss, and we grow into His very Image.

Here on earth the message of the permanent Truth, the transcendental Truth, has to be fulfilled, for God has chosen earth as His Field for Manifestation. The eternal Light has to be manifested here on earth, and we, all of us, have to become conscious instruments of God. We can be so if we have the inner cry, and this inner cry has to be the cry of a child. When a child cries for his mother, the mother, no matter where she is, comes running to him. The child may be in the living room or in the kitchen, but the mother comes running to feed him.

Similarly, when we have the inner cry, the spontaneous cry for Light and Truth, God out of His Infinite Bounty will show us the Light; and in that Light we will grow.

We shall fulfill God. While fulfilling God, we shall fulfill ourselves. Our only prayer to God is,

> Lead us from the unreal to the Real.
> Lead us from darkness to Light.
> Lead us from death to Immortality,
> O Lord Supreme!

IS THERE ANYTHING PERMANENT?

My Lord,
    How is it that there is nothing
    Permanent on earth?
    "Who told you so?
    Is jealousy not permanent on earth?
    Is doubt not permanent on earth?
    Is insecurity not permanent on earth?"
My Lord,
    True, they are.
    But when are You
    Going to make them impermanent?
    "Son, the moment the world wants Me to."
My Lord,
    Why do You blame the poor innocent world?
    After all, who created the world?

ATTACHMENT AND DETACHMENT

Trinity College, Dublin, Ireland
December 1, 1970

Attachment and detachment.
Detachment and attachment.

From the body we get the message of attachment.
From the soul we get the message of detachment.
The body is limited; hence the body wants to bind us and limit us. It wants to bind and limit our outer capacity and our inner potentiality.
The soul, in its potentiality and capacity, is limitless and endless. Therefore the soul wants to free us from the meshes of ignorance and liberate us from the bondage-night.

What is attachment? Attachment is the dance of our outer pleasure.
What is detachment? Detachment is the song of our inner joy.
Attachment ends in the prison-cell of frustration and destruction.
Detachment fulfills itself in the palace of Divinity and Immortality.

I am a fool if I consciously live in the physical. I am a greater fool if I constantly admire and adore my physical body. I am the greatest fool if I live only to satisfy the needs of my physical existence.
I am a wise person if I know that there is something called the soul. I am a wiser person if I care to see and feel my soul. I am the wisest person if I live in my soul and for my soul constantly and soulfully, unreservedly and unconditionally.
When we are attached to the body, we in no time become impulsive. When we are attached to the vital, we very soon become explosive. When we are attached to the physical mind, we ultimately become destructive.

But when we are in the body, detached, we consciously feel our aspiring consciousness. When we are in the vital, detached, we expand and widen our aspiring consciousness. When we are in the mind, detached, we supremely fulfill our unlimited consciousness here on earth.

Many people, unfortunately, mistakenly feel that attachment and devotedness are one and the same thing. But attachment means that we are in the finite and attached to the finite, and devotedness means that we devote ourselves to the Infinite and are liberated by the Infinite.

Here in Ireland, nearly a hundred years ago, a young aspirant named Margaret Noble left for India to become a famous disciple of Swami Vivekananda. This great Yogi had come to the West in 1889 to participate in the Parliament of Religions at the great World's Fair in Chicago. His spiritual stature was immediately recognized and he became famous overnight. When he went to England from the United States, Margaret Noble attended his talks and became his dearest disciple. He called her Nivedita, "one who is totally dedicated to the Supreme Cause."

Indian people are all admiration for what Nivedita did for India. She helped Indian women in infinite measure. She helped to awaken their slumbering consciousness so that they could envision themselves as divine instruments and grow into the perfect embodiments of aspiration, dedication and illumination for their Mother India. We Indians are filled with divine pride when we utter the name of Nivedita.

Her father was a clergyman, a great seeker and lover of God. On his deathbed, he said to his wife, "Don't stand in Margaret's way. If she wants to go to India, let her go." Margaret's mother had been very upset by her daughter's desire to leave Ireland for distant India, but at her husband's last request she helped Margaret and inspired her. Nivedita went to India and became India's veritable pride. Hers was the heart that knew no despair. Just before she passed behind the curtain of Eternity, she uttered under her breath, "The boat is sinking, but I shall see the sunrise."

I wish to offer my humble talk to the hallowed memory of Sister Nivedita, Margaret Noble of Ireland.

Detachment is misunderstood. We feel that if someone is detached he is indifferent. Spiritual seekers make the same mistake in thinking that when we want to be detached from someone, we must show him utter indifference, to the point of total neglect. This is not true. When we are indifferent to someone, we do nothing for him. We have nothing to do with his joy or sorrow, his achievement or failure. But when we are truly detached, we work for him devotedly and selflessly, and offer the results of our actions at the Feet of the Lord Supreme, our Inner Pilot.

It does not matter if the result is success or failure. If we are not at all attached to the results, we get an immediate expansion of consciousness. If we do not care for the fruit of our action, the Supreme rewards us in the Supreme's own Way.

Lord Krishna said, "Thou hast the right to act, but not to the fruits of action." The Upanishads declare, "Action cleaves not to a man."

If we work devotedly and selflessly, action does not bind us. There will be no difficulty in working for God's sake if we work without caring about the result. This is true detachment; this is spiritual detachment. When we can renounce the unlit, unaspiring action, we can enter into the divine action, which is our real life; and in this there is always perfection and fulfillment.

When we pay all attention to the material world and neglect the inner world, we starve the soul in us. The soul has to be brought to the fore. If we think that we can get infinite wealth from the material world, then we are totally mistaken.

Yagnayvalkya, the great Indian sage, had a wife whose name was Maitreyi. Yagnayvalkya wanted to spend the evening of his life in meditation and contemplation, so he decided to give away his earthly possessions. He asked Maitreyi if she wanted his riches. She asked, "Will your riches give me immortal life? Of what use to me are the things that cannot make me immortal?"

We need the material world, undoubtedly, but we cannot give all our energy to it. We feed our body three times a day. Unfortunately we do not have time to feed our soul even once a day. We, the seekers of the Infinite Truth, feed the body so that we can become perfect instruments of the soul.

The soul has Divinity, Eternity, Immortality. The soul wants to offer its world to the body. If the body becomes receptive, it will receive all that the soul has to offer. The body itself will echo and re-echo in the life of aspiration and dedication. It will march along as the most humble servitor of the soul. Its existence will be the existence of glory and divinity, divine service and supreme fulfillment.

We fulfill the Supreme on earth. He treasures us in His Heart's Heaven.

DIFFICULTIES

A woman
Finds it difficult
　To admit her insecurity.
　A man
Finds it difficult
　To admit his impurity.
　Poor earth
Finds it difficult
　To brave its sufferings.
　Rich heaven
Finds it difficult
　To hide its Treasures.
　The Supreme
Finds it impossible
　To overrule His Compassion.

THE PRISON-CELL OF MY ATTACHMENTS

I shall tell you one thing, therefore I have come
　to your door.
Mother, why does my mind commit the same
　mistake time and again?
Mother, will I get the flow of your
　blessing-smile in my teeming errors?
Striking my heart, do break asunder the
　prison-cell of all my attachments.

DIVINE DUTY AND
SUPREME REWARD

University of Glasgow, Glasgow, Scotland
December 2, 1970

God thinks of His Duty. God meditates on His Duty.

Man loves his reward. Man cries for his reward.

Duty performed unconditionally makes God happy, and that is what He does at every moment.

Reward gained effortlessly and constantly makes man happy, and that is what he always expects and lives for.

In our human duty we think of man in man. In our human duty we see man in man. That is to say, we love bondage in ignorance.

Our divine duty is to meditate on God in man. Our divine duty is to see God in man. That is to say, to love Divinity in Immortality.

Human duty begins with compulsion and very often ends in frustration and repulsion. Divine duty begins with inner necessity and ends in a flood of ecstasy.

Human reward and Divine reward. Human reward is the fleeting joy from an insignificant man. Human reward is the dying love from a weak human being.

Divine reward is the constant Joy, the everlasting Joy, that flows from God. Divine reward is the constant Love, the all-fulfilling Love, from God.

In our unaspiring life we perform duties and feel that duty is another name for labor. We also feel that duty is self-imposed, while reward is a most coveted pleasure. In our aspiring life, duty is voluntary. No, never is it obligatory. And reward is the energizing joy of selfless service. In our life of realization, duty is our divine pride, and reward is our glorious, transcendental height.

In our unaspiring life, and even in our aspiring life, we see that duty precedes reward. Duty comes first, then it is followed by reward. In the life of realization it is otherwise· reward first, then duty. How?

When God offers His Transcendental Height, His Highest Illumination, to someone, it means that God has already granted him full realization. God has accepted him as His chosen instrument. The very fact that God has accepted him as His chosen instrument indicates that he has already received the highest reward from God. Later God tells him about his duty: to love mankind, to help mankind, to serve the divinity in humanity, to reveal God the Eternal Compassion and to manifest God the Eternal Concern on earth, here and now.

Many years ago, an eminent Indian scientist, P. C. Ray, was a student at Edinburgh, here in Scotland. After completing his studies here, he went back to Bengal, India, to offer his knowledge to his Indian brothers and sisters. Now, it happened that one day somebody asked him how many children he had. He took out from his pocket a list of his children. Can you guess how many children he had? He had seventy-three children, in spite of the fact that he was a bachelor in the purest sense of the term! Then he said to his questioner, "Look, these are my children: seventy-three brilliant students. They are my true children. I am not married, but I consider them as my own children. They have given me the opportunity to serve mankind, and this is my duty. By serving these children of mine I perform my highest duty."

I wish to say that I am in the same boat, unmarried. I have a few hundred spiritual children. Out of His Infinite Bounty, God has showered His choicest Blessings upon my devoted head. My spiritual children give me abundant encouragement and opportunities, and meet with all my needs when I move around the world. This is my service, my dedicated service, and this is my bounden duty.

Today, at this august university, I am offering my selfless service. This is my last talk. My tour has come to an end. I have been away from New York for about a month. I have spoken at Cambridge, Oxford and other universities. I have just come from Switzerland, Wales, France and Ireland. Yesterday I was in Ireland and today I am here in Scotland. What am I doing? I am trying with utmost sincerity to be of service to sincere seekers. Each individual has the capacity to be of service to others. Only God can help us, and He always does. What we can do is to serve everybody here on earth. As a servant of God each individual has the capacity to serve mankind. Service is our matchless duty.

Duty and reward, from the spiritual point of view, go together. It is like the obverse and reverse of the same spiritual coin. Duty is man the aspiration, and reward is God the Realization and God the Liberation. Again, in reward is man's eternal journey, his ever-transcending journey; and in duty is God the ever-transforming, ever-manifesting, ever-fulfilling Reality here on earth, there in heaven.

> *Aum.*
> O Lord Supreme,
> Thou art my Mother.
> Thou art my Father.
> Thou art my Friend.
> Thou art my Comrade.
> Thou art the Knowledge-Light.
> Thou art the Inner Wealth.
> Thou art my All.

When we realize this Truth, we fulfill all our duties. There can be no greater duty than to realize the Inner Pilot.

Him to realize, Him to serve, Him to manifest on earth. For this we saw the light of day.

MY TASK

> I ask, my Lord Supreme, I ask:
> What is my task, what is my task?
> "My child, try and cry to change thy face,
> And tell the world My Name is Grace."
>
> Shall I succeed, can I succeed?
> "Why not, why not? My Breath shall feed
> Your life of love, devotion pure.
> Victory all-where when surrender sure."

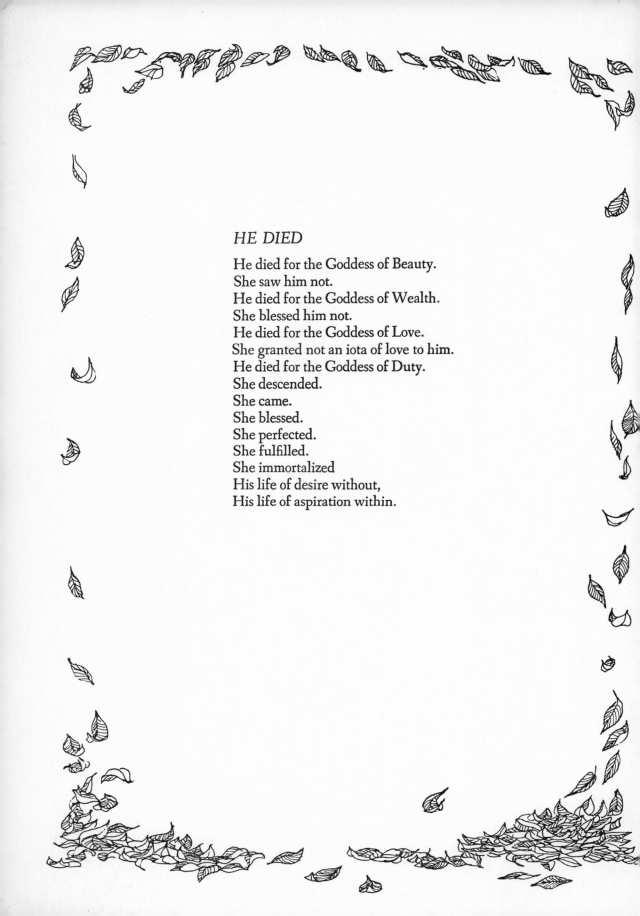

HE DIED

He died for the Goddess of Beauty.
She saw him not.
He died for the Goddess of Wealth.
She blessed him not.
He died for the Goddess of Love.
She granted not an iota of love to him.
He died for the Goddess of Duty.
She descended.
She came.
She blessed.
She perfected.
She fulfilled.
She immortalized
His life of desire without,
His life of aspiration within.

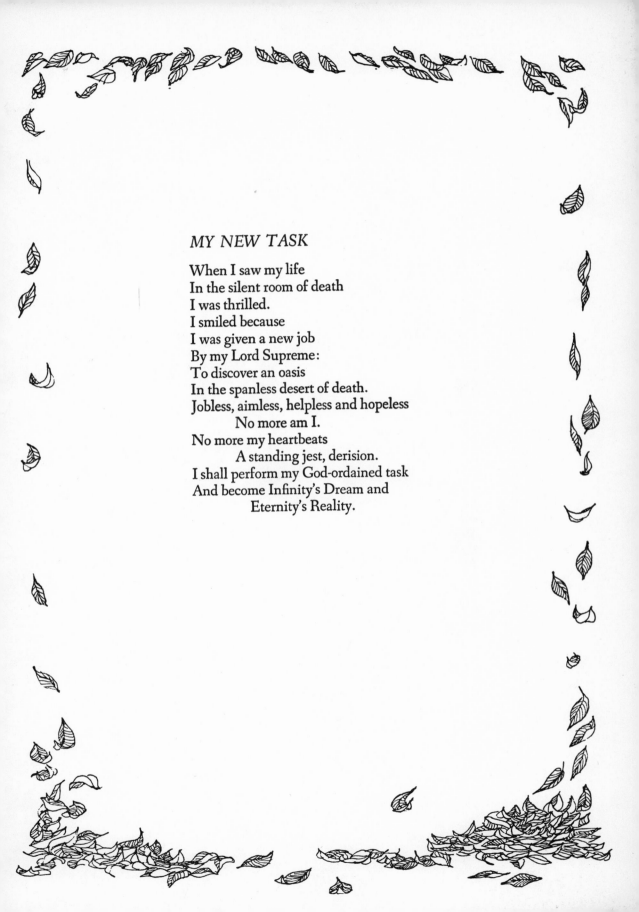

MY NEW TASK

When I saw my life
In the silent room of death
I was thrilled.
I smiled because
I was given a new job
By my Lord Supreme:
To discover an oasis
In the spanless desert of death.
Jobless, aimless, helpless and hopeless
        No more am I.
No more my heartbeats
        A standing jest, derision.
I shall perform my God-ordained task
And become Infinity's Dream and
        Eternity's Reality.

ABOUT THE AUTHOR

SRI CHINMOY was born in Bengal, India, in 1931. At the age of twelve he entered an ashram, or religious community, where he spent the next twenty years practicing meditation and intense spiritual disciplines. During this period, he underwent a series of profound religious experiences and achieved a state of enlightenment called God-Realization.

In 1964 he came to America to offer the fruits of his realizations to the aspiring Western consciousness. Since then he has established spiritual centers throughout the United States, Canada, Western Europe and Australia. He has published several dozen books on meditation and spirituality and has been invited to lecture at the world's great universities—including Oxford, Cambridge, Harvard, Yale and Tokyo. He conducts meditations twice a week for United Nations delegates and staff at the Church Center for the United Nations and the UN Headquarters in New York, and delivers the monthly Dag Hammarskjöld Lecture Series there. Daily meditations by Sri Chinmoy are broadcast by radio stations around the country, and a number of television stations air his early morning services on a regular basis.

The Supreme of All UNIONS

Om Shanti... I am a being of peace... I, the being of light... the living energy within the body... radiating... radiating thoughts... thoughts of peace... thoughts of lightness... of power... of mercy... of compassion... of love... pure thoughts of truth... I, a being of light... originally from a Land of Light... and, as I remember, I experience that Land of Light... I am a radiant star in a sky of golden-red light... surrounded in the eternal... in the peace of the Home... The land of Silence... there before me... coming closer... so beautiful... so attractive... such beautiful light... a tiny star yet the Ocean... waves of love flow between us... I the soul am bathed in the Ocean of Love... the Supreme Soul... my Mother... my Father... my Creator... I the soul in this ever-flowing Ocean of Light... Of Love... of Might... This One is revealing Himself with all His Beauty... within this Divine encounter I merge into that embrace of total love... that light into total union... with Baba, my beloved Father... and as I float down & take on my costume once more, that memory... that link... continues here... that relationship... I feel and experience my oneness with God... I and the Father are one... Om Shanti'